Deviant Behavior
and Social Control

ELEMENTS OF SOCIOLOGY
A Series of Introductions

Deviant Behavior and Social Control

S. Kirson Weinberg

Loyola University

WM. C. BROWN COMPANY PUBLISHERS
Dubuque, Iowa

SOCIOLOGY SERIES

Consulting Editors

Ann Lennarson Greer
University of Wisconsin—Milwaukee

Scott Greer
Northwestern University

Contents

Preface

ONE basic question in sociology pertains to the manner of society's control over its members. In this booklet my concern is with the popular query as to why some members escape this control and deviate from societal norms. Social deviation has been attributed to traits within the individual, to the nature of the act, and to a process of definition by which certain persons are designated as deviants. In this discussion we approach deviance as 1) the social influences that contribute to deviant behavior, 2) the impact of the particular form of deviant behavior on the group, community, or society, and 3) the social definition and re-action to the deviant whether by treatment, punishment, or prevention.

The group deviants develop mainly from learning and group affiliation on the one hand, and from social estrangement from conventional norms and persons on the other hand. Solitary deviants, however, develop mainly from a process of social es-trangement. To illustrate . . . I describe five forms of deviance which affect youth as well as adults: 1) the delinquent, 2) the drug addict, and 3) the homosexual, are group deviants, although they develop in different ways. 4) The mentally ill and 5) suicide are solitary deviants, who develop mainly by a process of estrangement.

Each deviant violates basic social norms. The delinquent violates the norms of the sanctity of private property and personal safety. The drug addict infringes upon the norms of personal propriety by ingesting forebidden chemicals. The homosexual breaks the rules of heterosexual consistency and gender identity. The mentally dis-ordered deviates from the standards of self-control and coherent communication. And the suicide trangresses the basic guideline of the preservation of life itself.

I acknowledge with thanks the proced-ural assistance by Mark Castegnaro, Lu-cille McGill, and William Frantz.

1 | Approach and Meaning

DEVIANT behavior refers to those actions which violate the norms of society and which are socially defined as reprehensible or threatening. Since deviant behavior disrupts societal standards, its authorized agencies and/or members react to control, punish or treat the deviant. When the detected deviant has been branded by judicial or other means and penalized or treated, he may be hindered in his future social acceptance and participation in law-abiding or conventional groups. In presenting the sequence of social processes which contribute to deviant behavior, we are concerned in this book 1) with the social processes and factors which contribute to the development of diverse forms of deviant behavior, 2) with the impact of predatory and nonpredatory deviants on society, and 3) with the manner by which society defines and aims to control and if possible change its predatory and nonpredatory deviants.[1]

TYPES OF DEVIANTS

Predatory deviants victimize and harm others, but nonpredatory deviants who violate the norms do not inflict harm or deprivation upon victims, except upon themselves, as among suicides. Predatory deviants consist of the delinquents and criminals including opiate addicts who turn to crime. Victimless deviants such as mentally ill, homosexuals and suicides, depart from societal norms which may make them objects of condemnation and ostracism. Our presentation will concentrate on both types of deviants.[2]

DEVIANT BEHAVIOR ARISES IN THE SOCIAL PROCESS

Deviant behavior is acquired as a result of the influence of social relations which characterize the social process. Through these social relations the deviant acquires his attitudes, orientations, and modes of behavior. When the person is attracted to and

1. Kai T. Erickson, *Wayward Puritans: A Study in the Sociology of Deviance* (New York: John Wiley & Sons, Inc., 1966).
S. Kirson Weinberg, *Social Problems in Modern Urban Society* (Englewood Cliffs, N. J.: Prentice-Hall Inc., 1970).
2. James F. Short, Jr. and Fred L. Strodtbeck, *Group Process and Gang Delinquency* (Chicago: The University of Chicago Press, 1965).
Bernard Barber, *Drugs and Society* (New York: Russel Sage Foundation, 1967).
Isidor Chernin et al., *The Road to "H"* (New York: Basic Books, Inc., Publishers, 1964).
Harold Finestone, "Narcotics and Criminality" *Law and Contemporary Problems.* (Winter, 1957) 22:69-85.
Edwin M. Schur, *Crimes Without Victims* (Englewood Cliff, N. J.: Prentice-Hall, Inc., 1965).

seeks acceptance from deviant associates his relationships are positive. From their informal tutelage, he learns his deviant behavior which is at variance with the norms of the larger conventional society. Many forms of group deviance such as delinquency, adult crime, drug addiction, and sometimes alcoholism, are learned in this way. This process is exemplified by the gang delinquent.

The gang delinquent becomes incorporated into the delinquent group in the very process of his socialized development. In fact, his peer relationships not only contribute to his delinquent behavior, but also affect his personal stability, which is bound up with peer acceptance. These peer relations reinforce his sex identity and masculinity, which is somewhat challenged by the female authorities about him: his mother and teacher. They orient him to his world and to himself. In the criminogenic community generations of criminals ranging from adult offenders to juvenile thieves coexist, and the juvenile learns criminal behavior from his associations on the street; this pathway is illustrated in the following excerpt:

Stealing in the neighborhood was a common practice among the children and approved by the parents. Whenever the boys got together they talked about robbing and made more plans for stealing. I hardly knew any boys who did not go robbing. The little fellows went in for petty stealing, breaking into freight cars and stealing junk. The older guys did big jobs like stick up, burglary and stealing autos. The little fellows admired the "big shots" and longed for the day when they could get into the big racket. Fellows who done time were big shots and looked up to and gave the little fellows tips on how to get by and pull off big jobs.[3]

The drug addict may also learn his addiction from his peer associates who introduce

him to the drug at "shooting" parties. When his withdrawal cravings appear and he requires the opiate to quiet them, his peers inform him of his addiction,—"getting hooked." His elaborate process of getting the drug involves him in an underground network in buying a very expensive substance in a criminal black market at exorbitant prices—the money for which he is compelled to steal.[4]

THE SOCIAL PROCESS IN INDIVIDUAL ESTRANGEMENT

The positive social process pertains to the deviant who learns his norms as a group participant. The negative social process refers to the social conflict and estrangement of the solitary deviant from his associates, parents, and/or his coworkers. His estrangement from any or all of these groups, his eventual isolation, and his failure to achieve a solitary solution of his personal problems and to enhance or redeem his self-esteem, may impel the deviant to the last resort of mental disorder or suicide.[5]

On this individual level, the person who becomes afflicted with a severe mental disorder has failed in his bid to solve his self-involved problems, so that his deviant behavior is evolved privately and not learned through interaction with his associates. For example, the youth who is in conflict with a domineering mother and who is rejected

3. Clifford R. Shaw, editor, *The Jackroller* (Chicago: University of Chicago Press, 1931).

4. David P. Ausubel, *Drug Addiction* (New York: Random House, Inc., 1966).

5. S. Kirson Weinberg, "Social Psychological Aspects of Schizophrenia," *The Sociology of Mental Disorders,* edited by S. Kirson Weinberg (Chicago: Aldine Publishing Company, 1967).
Edwin M. Schur, *Crimes Without Victims* (Englewood Cliff, N. J.: Prentice-Hall, Inc., 1965).

3

Table 1.1
Modes of Deviance By Presence or Absence of Victim

TYPE OF DEVIANT	MODE OF DEVIANT ACTIVITY	PRESENCE OF VICTIM
Delinquent	Theft Assault Arson Vandalism	Yes—directly other person
Drug Addict	Illicit Use of Drug	Yes—Indirectly: may rob or mug victim for money to buy drug
Homosexual	Illicit or Inverted Sexual Behavior	Predominantly Not, unless he forces others to submit sexually.
Mentally Disordered Person: Psychotic "Insane"	Bizarre behavior, may hurt himself	Largely Not, but may harm self or others
Suicide	Destroys or kills himself	Yes: Self

by his peers may strive to relate with his peers more effectively to regain his self-respect, but lacks the confidence to resist his mother or to fight his peers. Taunted, intimidated, and humiliated, he retreats into solitary pursuits away from the insults of others. In his isolation, he may behave strangely, indicative of a psychotic onset. As a consequence of his bizarre activities, he becomes socially defined as deviant and in need of psychiatric treatment.

Similarly, the individual who because of conflicts with and condemnation by his family, peers, finance, or work associates may, in desperation, attempt suicide as a last resort or he may break down.[6] For example, one person during a breakdown screamed so loudly he required psychiatric attention. He could not be quieted as he disclosed many deep fears. His brother brought him to a Veteran's Clinic for examination and arranged for an interview.

The next night, however, he got worse and in fright screamed so loudly that the family had to hospitalize him the next day to avert complaints of the neighbors.[7]

6. See James Wilkens, "Suicidal Behavior," *American Sociological Review*, (April, 1967) 32:2 pp. 286-298. Jack Douglass, *The Social Meaning of Suicide* (Princeton, N. J.: Princeton University Press, 1967).

7. S. Kirson Weinberg. *The Sociology of Mental Disorders*. Robert K. Merton, *Social Theory and Social Structure* (New York: The Free Press, 1957) pp. 134-147. See also, Robert K. Merton, "Social Structure and Anomie," *The Family, Its Function and Destiny*, ed. Ruth Anshen (New York: Harper & Row, Publishers, 1949) pp. 275-312. Marshall B. Clinard, *Anomie and Deviant Behavior* (New York: The Free Press, 1964) pp. 10-30. Albert K. Cohen, "The Sociology of the Deviant Act: Anomie and Beyond," *American Sociological Review* (February, 1965) 30:5-14. W. I. Thomas and Florian Znaniechi, *The Polish Peasants in Europe and America* (New York: Alfred A. Knopf, Inc., 1927).

Table 1.2

Types of Social Processes and Types of Deviants

ASPECT OF SOCIAL PROCESS	POSITIVE PROCESS	NEGATIVE PROCESS
1. Modes of Relationship	Association	Dissociation
2. Compatibility of Relationship	Consensus	Dissensus Conflict
3. Reaction of Associates	Approval and Acceptance	Disapproval and Rejection
4. Reaction of Prospective Deviant	Social Conformity and Participation: "Feeling of Belonging"	Withdrawal and Social Estrangement: "Feeling of Isolation and/or Rejection."
5. Acquisitions of Deviant	Group Imparts, and Deviant Learns Norms of Group	Deviant Renounces and/or Resists Norms of Group
6. Effect Upon Self-Esteem of Deviant	Raises Self-Esteem and Affirms Identity	Lowers Self-Esteem and Confuses Identity
7. Stability of Personality	Stable Enough to Acquire Norms by Group Acceptance	Unstable: Withdraws or is Rejected by Group
8. Function of Deviance	Provides a Collective Solution for Status or Provides Social Acceptance	Result of Failure to Find Solution for Personal Problems
9. Type of Deviant	Group Deviant: Delinquent, Criminal, Drug Addict	Solitary Deviant: Mentally Disordered, Suicide, Some Alcoholics

DEVIANCE AND THE CONTRA-CULTURE

The orientations, norms, rationalizations, techniques and values as the substantive content of the deviant group comprise its contra-culture.[8] The contra-culture as a sub-culture is in conflict and opposes the norms and values of the larger conventional society. Its illegal practices range from stealing through drug-addiction. Its values are inverted. Among criminals, competence in thieving is a criterion of prestige. The larger the amount stolen usually the higher one's status. Members of a contra-culture operate on the fringes of margins of society. They represent an in-group among themselves, who suspect and oppose conformist members of society as the out-group. They have

8. See Ruth S. Cavan, *Juvenile Delinquency* (Philadelphia: J. B. Lippincott Company, 1969). Milton Yinger, "Contra-Culture and Subculture" *American Sociological Review* (December, 1960) 25:6:625-635.

rationalizations to justify their behavior and to enhance their status. When the deviant initially is caught and lacks the rationalizations which would neutralize the stigma of his behavior or invert its importance, he feels stigmatized. Or when he seeks employment or social acceptance by conformist groups, he then may experience discrimination against him. But when he confines his associations to other deviants, he affirms his deviant identity.

The contra-culture tends to provide a collective solution for the problems of some deviants, whether these be problems of status, money, diversion and/or pleasure. In this respect, the members of a contra-culture differ from the solitary deviants who do not seek or at least cannot attain collective solutions for their personal problems.[9]

DEVIANCE AND SOCIAL DISORGANIZATION: THE DYNAMICS OF ANOMIE

Social disorganization in the community is indicated by the prevalence of deviant behavior. Social disorganization was defined by W. I. Thomas and F. Znaniechi as "the community's declining control" over its individual members. But this declining control may result from group as well as solitary forms of deviation. Thus community disorganization may result from the presence of contra-cultures among delinquents, adult offenders, drug addicts and prostitutes. These several subcultures are in conflict with the prevailing norms of conformistic behavior. This resulting "conflict of norms" which disrupts the consensus concerning appropriate behavior is social disorganization. Sutherland and Cressey have referred to this condition as "differential organization," because the members of the deviant groups conform to their respective norms.[10] The prevalence and persistence of the forms of deviance within a community occur because the conformist norms of the community cannot be enforced. A normlessness of behavior prevails within the community. The members of each contra-culture strive to fulfill their own needs at the expense of others in the community, with a consequent breakdown of the regulatory or control dynamisms of the community, which Durkheim referred to as an anomic condition.

SOCIAL FACTORS IN DEVIANT BEHAVIOR

Social factors are indicators that point to the social processes that contribute to the particular type of deviant behavior. Social factors include residential location, social class (including occupation, income, and education), age and sex, ethnicity and religion, marital status, and broken or intact home. The study of the influence of social factors upon deviant behavior indicates what relationships and influences specific factors have upon specific forms of deviance. For example, although juvenile delinquency increases markedly in the urban community, it is not sufficient to attribute urbanization in itself as a cause of delinquency, because a preponderant 95 percent of youths between 10 and 18 in the cities are not delinquent.[11] We would have to seek other factors such as sex, age, local community, father's occupation and education, recency of family settlement, and intact or broken home.

9. Albert K. Cohen, *Delinquent Boys* (New York: The Free Press, 1955).

10. Edwin H. Sutherland and Donald Cressey, *Principles of Criminology* (Philadelphia: J. B. Lippincot Company, 1966).

11. Sheldon and Eleanor Glueck, *Unraveling Juvenile Delinquency* (Cambridge: Harvard University Press, 1950).

From the ecological studies of the residential distribution of deviants in the urban community it was discerned that a residential pattern characterized several forms of deviant behavior such as delinquency, schizophrenia, drug addiction that are concentrated, as manifested by very high rates in the slums near the center of the city; and these rates declined with distance from the city's center to its circumference.[12] But these zonal patterns which represented radial processes of urban growth in a laissez-faire conception of society were not applicable to a planned urban community. Some slums in the city's center were rebuilt. In addition, the flight of people to the suburbs and the spread of physical deterioration to the very limits of the inner city changed this pattern. Thus, the ecological approach which studies the spatial distribution of man has also studied the residential distribution of deviants to ascertain the characteristics of the local communities which might have influenced these forms of behavior.

This ecological approach has been in part superseded by the influence of social class.[13] The factors of occupation, income, and education are clues and indicators of the position of individual deviants in the social structure; but they also provide the probability for influencing particular forms of deviance. Thus, the youthful male of the racial minorities in the slums whose family has recently settled in the city, who comes from a mother-headed family, will have higher probabilities of becoming delinquent than a youth of similar age of the suburbs whose father is a professional and whose family is intact. (Of course, in this particular instance, the latter boy may turn out to be delinquent and the former may not, depending upon other social processes.)

The analysis of social factors in deviant behavior pertains specifically to answering sociological questions: Why are rates of delinquency higher in one area than in another? Why have suicide rates increased among the youth? Have drug addiction rates increased among middle-class persons? These questions pertain to the study of definite social factors upon the particular types of deviance. This sociological orientation was emphasized by Durkheim in his study of suicide.[14] He questioned why suicide sustained its rates over a given period in some areas, why it was higher in one country than another, why it was lower in rural than urban areas. This type of perspective differed from the psychological vantage point which deals with what types of persons committed suicide.

PERSONALITY TRAITS

Many contemporary clinicians conceive of the deviant in terms of his distinct personality type. This view of personality as the basis of deviance reaches back into the late 19th and early 20th centuries and was usually attributed to biological and genetic sources. For example, the criminal was considered an evolutionary throwback to a lower species. The personality of the delinquent differed from that of the nondelinquent by lack of emotional stability and other pathological attributes. The drug addict at one time was considered a psycho-

12. Clifford R. Shaw and Henry D. McKay, *Delinquency and Urban Areas* (Chicago: University of Chicago Press, 1942).
Robert E. L. Faris and Henry W. Dunham, *Mental Disorders and Urban Areas* (Chicago: University of Chicago Press, 1939).
13. August B. Hollingshead and F. Redlich, *Social Class and Mental Illness* (New York: John Wiley & Sons, Inc., 1958).
14. Emile Durkheim, *Suicide* (New York: The Free Press, 1951).

path, distinct from the nonuser. The personality of the alcoholic was contrasted with that of the nonalcoholic. Since these forms of deviance are learned directly if informally, from peers and other associates, the function of personality tends to become subsidiary in their development.[15]

On the other hand, the solitary deviants whose behavior may result from defensive reactions in interpersonal conflict and isolation, may have personality differences distinct from those of the normal person. The psychotic, especially the schizophrenic, very likely has personality differences distinct from those of the nonschizophrenic. And the homosexual male also may have certain differences as contrasted with the heterosexual male.

The advent of psychoanalysis with its emphasis on early influences in basic personality provides insights for differentiating deviants from nondeviants. These clinicians emphasize that frustrations in early life influence, if not determine, the later onset of group and solitary deviant behavior such as delinquency. They contend that the later acceptance of deviant behavior stems from these early thwartings. For example, the Gluecks, Aichorn, Healy and Bronner regarded the child's frustrations incurred in early parent-child relations as a crucial determinant for his acceptance of delinquent behavior.[16]

On the other hand, sociologists emphasize that delinquency is learned from one's peers, and that the delinquent's early experiences are secondary. Although some youths may accept delinquent associates because of the hostility and aggression acquired from their relations with their parents, were delinquent associates not present in the area, very likely they would not have acquired these deviant patterns.

Early experiences may predispose the individual to unstable behavior, but these early experiences do not determine the learned deviant behavior unless he becomes attracted to deviant associates. In general, clinicians have not worked out why the individual will select one type of deviant behavior as distinct from other types of deviant behavior, except to emphasize that some of these persons may possibly be unstable.[17] On the other hand, sociologists have shown that some stable persons also may become deviant. For example, a person may become a drug addict in the process of medical treatment for a physical injury. One basic concern of the personality structure as it pertains to deviance is between the individual who is sufficiently stable to participate and become an accepted member of a deviant group and regard its practices as a solution to his personality problems, with the deviant who has become estranged from the group, who cannot form other associations and cannot solve his contemporary problems.

THE LOCUS OF DEVIANCE: DEPARTURE FROM THE NORM VERSUS SOCIETAL DEFINITION

Although societal definition is crucial in recognizing the reality of the deviance, the

15. See Edwin H. Sutherland, H. S. Schroeder, and C. L. Tordella, "Personality Traits and the Alcoholic," *Quarterly Journal of Studies on Alcohol* (December, 1950) 11:547-561.

16. Sheldon and Eleanor Glueck, *Unraveling Juvenile Delinquency;* August Aichorn, *Wayward Youth* (New York: The Viking Press, 1939); Wm. Healy and August Bronner, *New Lights on Delinquency and Its Treatment* (New Haven: Yale University Press, 1936).

17. See Harry Stack Sullivan, *Concepts of Modern Psychiatry* (Washington, D. C.: William Alanson White Foundation, 1945). S. Kirson Weinberg, *Society and Personality Disorders* (Englewood Cliffs, N. J.: Prentice-Hall, Inc., 1952).

mode of definition does not create the deviance nor does it explain the deviance. In temporal sequence, the societal norms, or standards are guidelines not only for conformist behavior, but also for the protection of the members of society. Those who deviate from these norms, depending upon their deviant activities, may or may not be officially designated or informally designated as delinquent; but the very violation of the norms may become instrumental in changing the standards of society and the ways of acceptable behavior. For example, in some families who practice father-daughter incest and escape detection, the very informal structure of the family changes into a kind of polygamy, regardless of whether it is so defined explicitly. When within a given community murder ensues and is not reported, but a vendetta starts between kin of the suspect and the victim, it revises the nature of their relationships and their respective degree of safety. When a community changes in its composition from being relatively free of crime to a condition of persistently high crime rates, the behavior of the residents changes regardless of whether the criminals are or are not caught. When the stress is upon the departure from the norm as being the locus of deviance the emphasis will turn to analyzing the modes of deviance and their effects on the group, community or society at large. When the focus of interest is on the definition of the deviant, then the attention of the study will be addressed to the comparative effects upon the deviant as a consequence of differing definitions.[18] Considerable attention has been directed to the diverse effects of socially defining and labelling the deviant, but relatively less interest has been concentrated upon the types of deviants who are discriminated against

as based upon their mode of deviance and its impact upon society. On this level we can observe the divergent societal reactions to predatory as distinct from nonpredatory deviants.

Thus, the locus of deviance inheres in the social process which in sequence includes as an integrated whole: (1) the modes of relationships which contribute to the development and onset of deviant behavior, (2) the modes of definitions that describe deviant behavior for those creating or controlling the definitions and stereotypes, and (3) the modes of relationships which sustain by penalties, or which aim and hope to reverse by treatment and prevention, the causal social influences of deviant behavior. To emphasize labelling or the causal process only is to substitute a fragment for the whole.

The Impact of the Nonpredatory Deviant

The nonpredatory deviant, such as the homosexual, the drug addict, or the mentally disordered person, and the suicide, has been regarded frequently with disgust and avoidance, but recently these attitudes have softened. His behavior is deviant because it is considered objectionable and repulsive, if not degrading. Thus the homosexual who would violate the sex norms of masculinity is viewed as a "pervert." The drug addict although frequently interrelated with the criminal, is considered weak-willed, with his insatiable desire for the drug, and hence is a "dope fiend." The psychotic such as the schizophrenic is downgraded by the very term of "insane" or "sick." The basic im-

18. Jack Gibbs, "Conceptions of Deviant Behavior: The Old and the New," *Pacific Sociological Review* (Spring, 1966).

plication of these connotations is that these persons as deviants are not acceptable as equals to "normal people," and their participation should be circumscribed, if they should not be sequestered from society.

However, the growth of tolerance and permissiveness in contemporary society has softened the stereotypes with respect to some deviants. Homosexuals have fought vigorously for understanding and for non-discrimination in employment. Similarly, former mental hospital patients, through their own organizations such as Recovery Incorporated, have gained more social acceptance and have improved the stigmatized image of themselves although, it continues to exist. The opiate addict has as a patient won more consideration than in the past for his claim to treatment as a sick person rather than punishment as a criminal.

The Impact of the Predatory Deviant

The sanctions and penalties imposed upon the predatory deviant are rituals for branding the deviant, but they may also represent secular ceremonies indicating that society has been able to control its deviants whose presence at large in the community demonstrates the helplessness of its enforcement agencies and of society itself. Thus trials as official rituals have a continuity with the reactions of potential victims who are immediately or potentially affected by the threat of the criminality.

The stereotypes of the predatory deviants may build up in a community, as the victims and potential victims who react defensively and communicate their fears to others. After hearing of neighbors and friends being robbed, beaten, burglarized or raped, citizens necessarily take protective steps.

They may not venture out at night, unless the trip is urgent; may double bolt their doors, build more secure steel fences, avoid certain parts of the community even during the daytime, and seek more effective police protection. The communication of fears about criminals may in extreme cases create attitudes of terror toward the stereotype of the criminal.

On the other hand, in areas where criminal behavior is infrequent, the attitudes towards the criminal may be abstract and removed, without the precautionary measures of the threatened area. Feeling safe from molestation of the robber or burglar or rapist, people may walk the streets at night, leave their doors unlocked, and visit different areas within the community.

Nonetheless, the awareness of criminal depredations is real, with the desire for sanctions and for the continuity of personal safety.

Of the different forms of crime, according to the National Opinion Research Center, white collar crimes involving deceit and fraud tend to be least frequently reported, while those involving the tangible stealing of foods, especially large items, and assault, are most frequently reported. But at least one out of three or more predatory cases of aggravated assault, robbery, and burglary is not reported.

Labelling the Deviant

From one point of view, the locus of deviance resides in the threat of the deviant action as it elicits the reactions of potential victims. From another broader view, according to Kitsuse, deviance is a process by which members of a group, community or society 1) interpret behavior as deviant, 2) define persons who so behave as certain kinds of deviants and 3) accord them the treatment considered appropriate to such deviants.[19]

The deviance then is not in the action *per se* but in the definition of the deviant and the extent to which the label of deviance can be applied effectively.[20] The locus of deviance from this perspective inheres in the ways people apply definitions to those who violate norms that the conformist community feels essential to their welfare or well-being. Their branding and penalizing deviants on the official level may be complex and dramatic.[21]

Stigma and the Negative Stereotype

The deviant stigmatized by law-abiding groups is presented by a negative stereotype that discredits and frequently ostracizes him. As an excluded outsider, he is perceived through this depreciating, generalized overlay which obscures his individuality. The "crook," the "nut," the "fag," the "dope fiend" are some derogatory references to stereotypes of diverse deviants. Such a stereotype represents a stigmatized image and has the following traits:

First, since the deviant role predominates over the other roles, the "ex-con" reference neutralizes other traits and roles of the individual. A criminal may be a doctor, lawyer or teacher, but the stigmatized role can overshadow the other roles. Second, the stereotype obscures individual differences of persons so categorized and presents them in a monolithic framework. Third, this stereotype overlay of the individual deviant deters the conventional person from perceiving and empathizing with him as a distinct individual, but instead, views him as an out-group member. Fourth, because of derogatory and hostile connotations of the

deviant stereotype, the conformistic person justifies his discrimination and penalties against him. Fifth, the deviant is consistently viewed as dehumanized, inferior, and unlike those persons in the accepted conventional in-group.[22]

The stigmatized deviant is further confined by societal reactions to his original or primary deviance. He encounters the thrust of disapproval and isolation to which he has to adjust. This discriminatory social process, which differs from the process of becoming a deviant, pertains to the societal penalties exacted from him. Lemert, who has differentiated primary and secondary deviance, has defined the two as follows:[23]

Primary deviation is assumed to arise in a wide variety of social, cultural and psychological contexts and at best has only marginal implications for the psychic structure of the individual; it does not lead to symbolic reorganization at the level of self-regarding attitudes and social roles.

Secondary deviation is deviant behavior, or social roles based on it which becomes means of defense, attack, or adaptation to the overt and covert problems created by the societal reaction created by the primary deviation. In effect, the original causes of the deviation recede and give way to the central importance

19. John I. Kitsuse, "Societal Reaction to Deviant Behavior: Problems of Theory and Method," *Social Problems,* (Winter, 1962) 9:3:256-258.

20. Howard S. Becker, *The Other Side: Perspectives on Deviance* (New York: The Free Press, 1964) pp. 1-9.

21. Kai T. Erickson, *The Wayward Puritans: A Study of the Sociology of Deviance* (New York: John Wiley & Sons, Inc., 1966) pp. 11-23. See also Erving Goffman, *Stigma* (Englewood Cliffs, N. J.: Prentice-Hall, Inc., 1963) pp. 4-10.

22. See S. Kirson Weinberg, "Aspects of the Prison's Social Structure," *American Journal of Sociology* (March, 1942) 47:5:717-727.

23. Edwin M. Lemert, "Social Structure, Social Control and Deviation," *Anomie and Deviant Behavior,* ed. Marshall B. Chnard (New York: The Free Press, 1964) p. 82.

of the disapproving, degredation and isolating reactions of society.

Schwartz and Skolnick devised an experiment to ascertain the effects of imprisonment on one's chances of securing employment. They sought the reactions of 25 employers (who did not know it was an experiment) to three applicants for unskilled work. The first applicant was an exprisoner, the second was acquitted for a crime, and the third had no criminal record. Nine employers agreed to hire the person without a criminal record, but only one employer was willing to hire the applicant with the prison record.[24] In brief, this discrepancy indicated the onus of the stigma against an exprisoner, even for unskilled work.

The former prisoner, like other deviants, may have to restrict his activities. Even if he may achieve a useful and respected role, his past imprisonment can become a "skeleton" in his closet which may haunt him. The negative brand of the former prisoner or of the former mental hospital patient (regarded as having been insane), or of the drug user, may obstruct his social participation and effect discrimination in employment. This sham can contribute to former prisoner's reversion to crime, or to the relapse of a former patient. In this sense, the persistence of the deviant label can reinforce deviance by narrowing or closing the person's options to conventional behavior. Such intolerance is more intensely expressed to the lower-class than middle-class persons. For example, an individual who served his term of imprisonment for income tax evasion was able to resume his place on the board of directors of a community recreation center. On the other hand, an exprisoner who had been sentenced for robbery was unable to get a job through a particular agency.

The Counterlabel

Although various kinds of deviants are branded in a derogatory way which leads to discrimination in jobs and social ostracism, these deviant groups counterlabel themselves as the equivalent of "underdogs," and feel that they have been victimized by an oppressive authority. They argue that they or their practices are "misunderstood" and that their rights as persons should be safeguarded.

Homosexuals, as nonpredatory deviants, liken themselves to members of a minority group who are penalized for practices which harm no one, who are discriminated against in jobs, who are impeded by attempts to blackmail homosexuals in sensitive jobs such as the foreign service. They object to the secrecy and shame with which homosexuality is regarded.

Some prostitutes too have claimed that their rights to a livelihood have been disrupted. They justify the practice of prostitution as a service to society. They claim that they are victimized by the police and other enforcement personnel. They may regard prostitution as a practice that should be legalized. They, too, place themselves in the category of "underdogs" whose rights should be heeded.

Rebellious prisoners in Attica, a maximum security prison in New York State, who protested that they were treated unjustly and were denied certain rights, regarded themselves as "underdogs." These offenders include murderers and thieves who deprived their victims of elemental rights during their own predatory experience. Admittedly, no paragons of virtue, they felt strongly

24. Richard Schwartz and Jeane H. Skolnick, "Two Studies of Legal Stigma" *Social Problems* (Fall, 1962) 10:133-138.

that they should be accorded treatment and care consistent with the tenets of a humane and democratic society. Thus, predatory deviants who are denied liberty in prison, for the protection of law-abiding citizens resort to the rationale that society should not abuse or deprive them of their just rights.

The group deviant from his vantage point, however, is a member of an in-group, opposed to or distinct from the larger conventional society. The very opposition characterizing group deviates, activates the dynamics of conflict in the conventional out-group with a logic of polarity and a rhetoric of the out-group inferiority. The drug addict refers to the nonuser as a "Square-John," the delinquent characterizes his victim as dishonest or as stupid, a "pigeon" or as small, a "punk," the confidence man has his "mark" or his "sucker," the homosexual being less predatory as "gay" considers himself distinct from the heterosexual "straight." The group offender, by renouncing or opposing the conventional group, tends to bolster his own identity. The solitary deviant lacks the morale for a persistent rhetoric about a hostile conventional society, although his hostility to the conventional outside exists.

Table 1.3

Views of Three Approaches to Deviance

Approach	Essential Views of Deviance
I. SYMBOLIC INTERACTIONISM: "Social Learning Theory"	1. Deviance arises from informal social learning by relations with deviant associates.
	2. Concern is with deviant behavior as norm violation.
	3. Concern is with controlling the dynanisms of social relations to reorganize society.
II. STRUCTURAL-FUNCTIONALISM: "Anomie Theory"	1. Deviance arises from discrepancy between cultural goals, e.g., success, and lack of institutional means to attain these goals, with a recourse to illegitimate means in a context of anomie of means.
	2. Concern is with deviant behavior as norm violation.
	3. Concern is with consistency between cultural goals and institutional means or opportunities to attain these goals.
III. NEO-SYMBOLIC INTERACTIONISM "Labelling Theory"	1. Deviance arises as a consequence of societal definition by people or agencies in dominant positions.
	2. Concern is with deviant behavior as a result of societal definitions.
	3. Concern is with greater tolerance for and acceptance of nonpredatory deviants and more systematic tolerance for susceptible deviants and former institutional deviants.

DEVIANT BEHAVIOR AND THE URBAN COMMUNITY

The urban community is the locus where the varied forms of deviance concentrate. Since the United States is essentially an urbanized society, the modes of deviation are influenced largely, if not predominantly, by this mass-industrial-urban civilization. The majority—over 70 percent—of people reside in and around the metropolitan areas; most of our factories, our commerce, and our innovations, arise in the metropolitan sectors of society, particularly the large metropolitan areas. It is in urban society too that the forms of deviation abound.[25]

Furthermore, most sociological studies are concerned with deviants in urban communities. On the one hand, this makes us more knowledgeable about, and perhaps more effective in coping with, urban deviants. On the other hand, although deviants exist in small towns and rural communities in lesser frequency than in urban communities, we have comparatively little knowledge about them. Deviance in small towns and rural areas is mentioned because minimal attention is directed to the prevalence of deviance in these communities, which despite their size are increasingly influenced by the mass-urban society. Also, it has been emphasized by some sociologists that the varied types of deviance, such as delinquency, adult crime, drug addiction, mental disorder and suicide, were inherent in urban disorganization from which the idealized small town and rural sectors were exempt. But urban forms of deviance exist in rural as well as in urban areas, if in lesser degree.

Problems in the Control of Deviance

The control of the different forms of deviance exist within the processes of contemporary American Society, as do the measures of repression, rehabilitation and prevention. The rates for different forms of deviance reflect the functions and stresses within contemporary society. Consequently, since the forces and functions of urbanized society remain relatively similar except perhaps for the more intense disorganization within the inner city, yet the different forms of deviance, including delinquency, drug addiction, psychoses and suicide, reflect these mildly fluctuating social influences. Unless society changes drastically, disorders should also fluctuate but not change drastically. Societal stresses which have focussed on contemporary youth have resulted in marked increases in rates of mental disorders and suicide.[26]

The present measures of control cannot achieve the drastic reduction of any form of deviance unless the basic social processes within society change and/or unless the modes of formal social control, whether by repression, rehabilitation, or prevention, counteract the processes contributing to the forms of deviance. None of these changes is evident in sufficient force and scope.

First, physical deterioration and social disorganization have become more widespread within the inner city, and in some instances have spread to the suburbs.

Second, personnel working with deviants have become more effectively trained and increasingly professionalized. Law enforcement personnel receive more training than ever before. Therapists and researchers have increasingly focussed their interests on deviants, especially predatory deviants.

25. See Daniel Glaser, ed., *Crime in the City* (New York: Harper & Row, Publishers, 1970).

26. S. Kirson Weinberg, *Social Problems in Modern Urban Society* (Englewood Cliffs, N. J.: Prentice-Hall, Inc., 1970).

Third, the increased sociological and psychological research into many forms of deviant behavior has contributed to deeper understanding of their causes and the possibilities for control. In addition, the federal and local governments have accumulated research data on the trends of delinquency, adult crime, drug addiction, alcoholism, mental disorders, especially psychoses, and suicides.

The effectiveness of law-enforcement agencies in suppressing predatory deviants has been rendered more challenging by the relatively thin line existing between individual rights and police authority. Within a democratic framework individual rights must be respected, their violation makes law-enforcement officers legally liable, and with evidence, culpable, a situation which makes arrest and conviction more difficult. By contrast, the reaction of government of Ghana, West Africa, (c. 1960) to a wave of automobile thefts was to arrest every person remotely suspected of being an automobile thief through the law of preventive detention. As a result, car thievery dropped by about 80 percent in several weeks. Although a society of this latter type may reduce crime, it may also suppress individual liberties and expose citizens to arrest by the arbitrary whims of the state. Because of guarantees of liberties to citizens in a democratic society, the predatory deviant as a suspect is also protected.[27] To achieve effective law enforcement, and to rehabilitate deviants to a normal way of life detection and conviction must be effected within a democratic framework.

The sociological goals of coping with social problems of deviance are unlike those of the biologist who can strive to eliminate the germ-carrier of a disease and immunize persons who are exposed to the germ. The sociologist must regard deviance as emerging from the social process and the warp and woof of society. His realistic and modest aspiration is to reduce the scope of defiance to controllable dimensions. Nonpredatory forms of deviance such as homosexuality could be accorded greater societal tolerance and acceptance in their vocational and other useful pursuits.

Among the action systems to reduce predatory deviance are the experimental preventive programs. The several preventive plans designed to reduce juvenile delinquency have not been notably successful, despite the apparent soundness of their rationale. The preventive educational projects to avert drug addiction seemed to have a ricochet affect: The children who were exposed to preventive education about drugs became more curious about the drugs and hence were more apt to try drugs than the children who had no preventive education.[28]

The strategy of prevention that began with the use of the community concept as a point of departure for preventing delinquency has spread to psychiatry, psychology, and in part to criminology. In following this rationale it has resulted in a decline in forcibly retaining deviants within institutions and a rising trend in treating deviants by trained personnel in the community and in appropriate agencies or clinics. This community approach has been moderately effective in readapting deviants. Some of these were not ready for community adaptation despite the help received, as we shall elaborate in subsequent chapters dealing with types of deviants. This approach has been encouraged in large

27. Ibid.
28. See Chapter III.

measure by some lay groups, because it has been demonstrated to be cheaper than housing deviants within institutions.[29]

For Further Reading

Becker, Howard. *The Outsiders.* New York: The Free Press, 1963.

Presents the bases of the labeling aspects of deviant behavior.

Clinard, Marshall B. *The Sociology of Deviant Behavior.* New York: Holt, Rinehart & Winston, Inc., 1968.

Developed and applied the conception of deviant behavior.

Rushing, William A. ed. *Deviant Behavior and Social Process.* Chicago: Rand McNally & Company, 1969.

This anthology describes examples of deviant behavior and some modes or research in studying such behavior.

Weinberg, S. Kirson. *Social Problems in Modern Urban Society.* Englewood Cliffs, N. J.: Prentice-Hall, Inc., 1970.

Analyzes deviant behavior from the perspective of social action.

Winslow, Robert W. *Society in Transition.* New York: The Free Press, 1970.

Applies the classical sociological theories of Marx, Weber, and Durkheim to the study of social deviance.

29. Stephen E. Goldston, ed., *Concepts of Community Psychiatry,* Public Health Service Publication No. 1319 (Washington, D. C.: U.S. Government Printing Office, 1965).

2 | Juvenile Delinquency

JUVENILE delinquency is one of the pervasive social afflictions of an urban civilization. Although it is concentrated among children and youth of the lower socioeconomic classes who inhabit the urban slums, it extends through the middle classes though in lesser percentages. Juvenile delinquency is not merely antisocial behavior, it is essentially illegal conduct; the juvenile delinquent has violated a law or is accountable to the law, and as specified by the particular state is under a given age, usually under 18. The categories of delinquent behavior include: 1) stealing, 2) vandalism or destruction of property, 3) assault, 4) sexual deviance, 5) truancy from home or school.[1] These categories of illegitimate behavior, however, have been revised in some states such as Illinois, where felonies or serious crimes are differentiated from the minor offenses which do not victimize others, such as truancy, vagrancy, promiscuity.[2]

The delineation of delinquency as an act differs from the process by which a child or youth is defined as a delinquent. The juvenile culprit must first be detected and apprehended, then tried in juvenile court where his appearance as well as his conviction are duly recorded. Juveniles from different classes and ethnic groups are treated in distinct ways. The lower class lad who comes from a broken home with his mother as his sole parent may be brought more readily before the juvenile court than the upper middle class youth whose father can convince authorities that he will refer the boy as a social problem to a psychiatrist. Thereby the boy avoids a court appearance. When youths of Jewish or of Catholic faith have agencies intercede in their behalf, the judge can entrust them to the custody of these agencies for rehabilitation. On the other hand, boys of other ethnic or religious groups without interceding agencies are tried before and sentenced by the juvenile court. In general, although a higher proportion of lower class offenders are arrested than middle class youths, a still higher percentage of lower class boys are also summoned to the juvenile court than are upper middle class offenders.

1. Sol Rubin, *Crime and Juvenile Delinquency* (New York: Oceana Publications, Inc., 1958) Chapter 2.
2. Ruth S. Cavan, *Juvenile Delinquency* edition (New York: J. B. Lippincott Company, 1964) 14: 23-28. Wendell Huston, Compiler, Social Welfare Laws of the Forty-Eight States (Seattle: Wendell Huston Company, 1973).

Juvenile court officers can influence the manner of the delinquent's classification, the seriousness of the charges and the treatment, by recognizing that the appearance of some first offenders in court has adverse effects upon them. Consequently, the officer may try to clarify the nature of the offense at the police station, where he meets with the offender, his parents, and the victim. This officer may resolve the situation by admonitions to the juvenile about stopping his illegitimate and predatory activities, by advice to his parents with regard to more stringent control, and about probable restitution to the victim. By this police station arrangement, the youth is spared from appearing in court.[3]

In describing the processes of delinquency in this chapter, we shall cover 1) the extent of officially reported delinquency, with some mention of delinquency that is not thus reported, 2) the emergence of delinquency in the social process, as a peer group experience and as an estrangement from conventional norms, 3) the social factors and personality traits pertinent to delinquency, and 4) the modes of social control by techniques of custody, rehabilitation, and prevention.

THE EXTENT OF JUVENILE DELINQUENCY

Delinquents register high rates of arrests for thefts involving force or the threat of force. In 1966 youths under 18 comprised 22.9 percent of all the arrests: 33.1 percent of all arrests in the suburbs, 22.7 percent of all arrests in the city, and 19.7 percent of all arrests in rural areas. Respective percentages for youths under 18, among all arrests for combined major felonies including homicide, forcible rape, robbery, aggravated assault, burglary, larceny—theft and

auto theft, were 50.7 percent in the cities, 53¼ percent on the suburbs, and 36.6 percent in the rural areas.[4]

Youthful offenders also constitute a very high proportion of total persons arrested for the destruction of property, including vandalism, (78 percent), arson, (71.5 percent), and for buying, receiving or possessing stolen property, (38 percent). Their inevidence among all arrests for sex offenses, except forcible rape and prostitution was 24.5 percent, for use of drugs was 14.4 percent and for violation of liquor laws 29.2 percent.[5]

Apparently, children under 12, and even under 14, participated far less in stealing and destruction of property, than boys aged 15 through 17. These arrests include females as well as males. Moreover, except for rape, female delinquents were markedly similar to males in types of arrests. In fact females accounted for a higher proportion of total arrests than males do: 44.9 percent to 20.6 percent.[6]

Although the officially recorded statistics are our principal concern as an indication of the extent of delinquency, it should be pointed out, however, that many delinquents are not detected, not reported, and not defined as delinquents. This information has been derived from self-reported surveys in which students of high schools and grade schools have been asked to report anonymously about the types of of-

3. Irving Piliavin and Scott Briar, "Police Encounters With Juveniles," *American Journal of Sociology* (1964) 70:206-214.

4. Federal Bureau of Investigation, U.S. Department of Justice, *Uniform Crime Reports for the United States, 1966*, (Washington D. C.: U.S. Government Printing Office, 1967) pp. 125, 126, 134, 142, 143.

5. *Ibid.*

6. *Ibid.*

fenses they have committed, whether or not they have been caught.

In 1946, the results of a five year study of 114 boys in Massachusetts reported that of 6, 416 infractions, only 95 were reported; this amounts to less than 2 percent of the total. In 1972, a national survey reported that less than 3 percent of the offenses committed are detected by the police. Thus the vast number of offenses remain unknown to the police, but it should be emphasized that the overwhelming proportion of these offenses were minor.

Short and Nye have reported that while many boys have committed unrecorded minor offenses, relatively few have perpetrated serious offenses.

In a study of a sample of 3,100 male and female adolescents in Illinois to ascertain the extent of their legal infractions, the research staff of the Institute for Juvenile Research found too that the overwhelming proportion of offenses were minor although

some offenses were far higher than the percentages found by Short and Nye.

DELINQUENCY AND THE SOCIAL PROCESS

Delinquency is a Function of a Group Experience

Although the delinquent may be judged in the court in terms of his offenses as a discrete individual, his delinquent activities, especially stealing, very frequently are expressed as group experiences. For example, in 1930, Shaw and McKay found that of 5,480 delinquents, 81.9 percent were arrested in groups; and of 4,663 delinquents arrested for stealing, 89 percent were arrested in cliques of two or more boys.[7] Glueck found that 70 percent of

7. Clifford R. Shaw and Henry D. McKay, "Social Factors in Juvenile Delinquency," *Causes of Crime* (Washington D. C.: U.S. Government Printing Office, 1931).

Table 2.1

Unrecorded and Recorded Delinquencies Among Adolescents—By Percentages

	UNRECORDED		RECORDED
	IJR* Sample (Boys & Girls)	Short & ** Nye Group (Boys)	Correctional** School (Boys)
Taking Little Things	56	60.6	91.8
Taking Things Worth More ($20 or More)	16	($50 or more) 5.6	90.8
Using Strong Arm Methods to get Money	13	6.3	67.7
Rode in Stolen Car	10	14.8	75.2
Broke into Home or Store or Place to steal	13	. .	. .

*Institute for Juvenile Research, *Juvenile Delinquency in Illinois* (Chicago: Department of Mental Health, 1973), pp. 38-40.
**James F. Short Jr. and F. Ivan Nye, "Extent of Unrecorded Juvenile Delinquency," *Journal of Criminal Law, Criminology and Police Science,* (1958) 49:297.

1,000 delinquents were influenced by other delinquents.[8] In brief, the peer associates have a significant influence upon youths who become delinquents

The crucial clue is that the juvenile learns his delinquency from associates whose acceptance he seeks. By those selective relations or differential associations, his peers impart rationalizations, orientations, and techniques which encourage or impel truancy, malicious mischief, vandalism, theft, and gang fights.[9] They may encourage his alienation from or intensify his conflict with the school, family, and conventional community. They may demand loyalty to his associates above that owed to the laws of the larger, conventional society. Although the delinquent realizes that he is violating the law, he may, in fact, believe that his loyalties are to his peers. Frequently his attachment to his peers is absolute and uncritical. In his provincial outlook, his block or his neighborhood is his social world in scope, and those outside its territorial boundaries, or "turf," are considered strangers, even hostile foes, as is evident in some youths' hostility toward rival delinquent gangs.

In a tightly cohesive gang, the individual member may be forced to conform to its rules and norms, while his lack of conformity may lead to injury or death. For example, one delinquent who avoided a planned theft in company with his associates, was sought out in his home and beaten severely in his living room in his mother's presence.

The Delinquent Subculture is a Contra-Culture

Since the delinquent group is in conflict with law-abiding society, its norms of behavior and values contrast with and oppose the conduct and norms of that society. The delinquent subculture has been characterized as having an inverse value system to that of conventional state of civilization: it opposes respect for property, rejects nonviolence or minimal violence, as well as established authority and its agents such as the police. Thus, delinquents acquire the rationalizations and techniques to justify predatory behavior against society, like stealing, destruction of property, assaulting their victims or members of rival gangs.[10] Their participation in law-breaking activities evokes praise from their delinquent associates but would stigmatize them by law-abiding youths. Their commitment to and incarceration in correctional institutions because of their illicit activities tends to heighten their status among their companions. But values which delinquents learned from their companions develop within a framework of meanings, morality, rationalizations, and offenses. By participating in law-breaking activities, they become increasingly alienated from the hostile to conventional norms, isolated from law-abiding people, more involved and cohe-

8. Sheldon and Eleanor Glueck, *Unraveling Juvenile Delinquency* (New York: The Commonwealth Fund, 1950).

9. James F. Short, Jr., Ramon Riveria and Ray A. Tennyson, "Perceived Opportunities Gang Membership and Delinquency," *American Sociological Review* (February, 1950) 30:56-57; *Social problems.* (Fall, 1959) 6:2:108-117; Solomon Kobrin "The Conflict of Values, in Delinquency Areas," *American Sociological Review* (1951) 16: 653-661. Also S. Kirson Weinberg, "Juvenile Delinquency in Ghana," *Journal of Criminal Law Criminology, and Police Science.* (December, 1964) 55:471-481.

10. See Lewis Yablonsky, *The Violent Gang* (Baltimore: Penguin Books, 1966); Richard A. Cloward and Llyod E. Ohlin, *Delinquency and Opportunity* (New York: The Free Press, 1960).

sive in their associations with delinquent companions. Sheldon and Eleanor Glueck point out that over 95 percent associated with other delinquents.[11]

The rationale of delinquent groups is implicit in their activities. Their subculture is not a written or codified culture, though it is in fact described and classified by sociologists. The delinquents know to what norms they are to conform and what practices they are to observe. They adhere to a subculture on the basis of the approval and disapproval by others, and not because of written laws. The values and norms of their subculture are not unlike those of a folk culture, insofar as they are transmitted verbally and by example rather than by formal instruction and written tutelage, as Matza has indicated:

The code of the delinquency is relatively latent. It is not written . . . nor is it well verbalized. Its precepts are neither codified nor formally transmitted. Rather they are inferred from action which obviously includes speech. An ideology of delinquency in the sense of a coherent viewpoint is implicit in delinquent action but this ideology is not known to delinquents.[12]

Cohen contends that delinquent behavior is a short-run, nonutilitarian form of activity.[13] Delinquents can bolster their status because of values inverse to middle class, conformistic standards. But empirical study reports that delinquents may not necessarily feel deprived in status, and that they are motivated by the values which they acquire from the peers, without concern about principles and standards of middle class boys.[14] They act out practices because of their isolation from the middle class conformist examples. This effort by Cohen to derive the motivation for delinquency from a status-solution effort among lower class boys, is pursued further by Miller, who

hypothesized from hundreds of interviews with lower-class boys, that the way they approached their "focal concerns" contributed to their delinquency.[15]

These focal concerns include 1) trouble, 2) toughness, 3) excitement, 4) fate, 5) smartness, and 6) autonomy. Trouble meant the youth's facing of agencies of society when apprehended in law violating behavior. The lower-class individual's capacity was tested by the way he could cope with police agencies when he did violate the law, by his ability to maintain his reputation with peers and other significant persons.

Toughness referred to the person's physical skills, masculinity, and fearlessness in dealing with his problems, as contrasted with an effeminate and cautious approach to challenges. "Excitement" emerged from orgies or escapes. "Fate" referred to the direction of one's life as determined by forces beyond the person's control, perhaps expressed in gambling or in other risk behavior. "Smartness" was interpreted as the ability to "con" people out of things rather than to be duped oneself. "Autonomy" referred to the youth's capability with respect to the amount, severity, and basis for control, or his evasion of control by others. The importance of Miller's emphasis is his proposed explanations of delinquency in

11. Sheldon and Eleanor Glueck, *Unraveling Juvenile Delinquency.*
12. David Matza, *Delinquency and Drift* (New York: John Wiley & Sons, Inc., 1964) p. 51.
13. Albert K. Cohen, *Delinquent Boys.*
14. See S. Kirson Weinberg, "Shaw-McKay Theories of Delinquency in Cross-Cultural Context," *Essay in Honor of Henry McKay*, edited by James F. Short, Jr. (Chicago: University of Chicago Press, forthcoming).
15. Walter Miller, "Lower Class Culture As a Generating Milieu of Gang Delinquency," *Journal of Social Issues* (April, 1958) 14:3:5-19.

terms of lower class rather than middle class values. Since delinquency also appears among middle class youth, Miller leaves unexplained the motivational sources of delinquency in the middle stratum of society.

Ohlin and Cloward analyzed delinquent subculture in terms of opportunity systems, which they classified as theft, gang fighting, and drug usage.[16] Delinquents who unequivocally accept thieving practices usually develop in areas with homogeneous criminal cultures. They strive to emulate successful hoodlums who have considerable money and prestige, role models who demonstrate power in the community, and are admired as "big shots." These criminals are symbols of success and power attained by illegitimate means; they demonstrate their power and influence by going about free, although known crimes are attributed to them. In other areas, where norm-abiding and norm-violating patterns coexist, gang conflicts may result as one means of sustaining the reputation or "rep" of the delinquent youths. Cloward and Ohlin contend that youths who fail in their conventional pursuits and are rejected by delinquents retreat into drugs, to escape their "double failure." It may of course be argued that retreatism as a personal escape dynamism may assume several outlets, such as flight, violence, and even theft. On the other hand, it may be demonstrated that some drug addicts acquire their insatiable, binding habit from the informal tutelage and pressure of their peers, without motivation of failure.

The delinquent subculture, though opposed to the larger conventional culture, nevertheless has continuity with it. Cohen has perceived the delinquent subculture in terms of inverted values with respect to the middle society. Miller has viewed this subculture as emerging from and continuous with the way of life of the lower class. Matza, too, has traced the continuity between the delinquent subculture and the larger culture, and has noted their subsurface convergence, as between the masculine cowboy of the mass media and the masculinity of the delinquent, the manifest aggression in the spy stories, the pervasive use of firearms reported in the newspapers, and many predatory forms of behavior seen and heard in the mass media, including the pervasive aggression among slum youths who incorporate these influences received from the mass media, using them to rationalize and to "normalize" their own behavior. The discontinuity that the delinquents do not see is the difference between daily reality and the fantasy expressed in the media.[17] The use of firearms to murder in a movie may be sloughed off by an audience, but in real life it is an unusually traumatic experience for many people. The capers and illegal antics in the spy movies of James Bond are highly entertaining, but when somewhat similar antics were used by a government agent in this country against some citizens these illegal "dirty tricks" aroused intense disapproval by most citizens. Although forms of aggression in the mass media are continuous with those in the delinquent group, they are incongruous when contrasted with behavior patterns among youths and especially adults in the middle classes. Furthermore, delinquents as juveniles also overlook the discontinuity in behavior patterns between adults and juveniles, because of their discontinuous age-roles.

16. Cloward and Ohlin, *Delinquency and Opportunity*.
17. David Matza, *Delinquency and Drift*.

Estrangement from Conventional Groups and Values

The delinquent not only moves toward deviant associates, he also moves away from law-abiding institutions and persons. Initially he may be in conflict with his family, should his father or mother want him to continue his attendance and interest in school, or they should try to dissuade him from associating with his delinquent peers. Frequently, he is compelled to associate with the boys who are residents of the block or of the multi-unit apartment building where he lives. If he tries to avoid them, they may beat him, trick him, taunt him, and even in extreme cases, try to kill him. Within these circumscribed borders, he builds his social world, a milieu that may be excluded from the conventional society of which he does not feel himself a part.

One basic conventional institution is the school. To the middle-class, nondelinquent child, the school is regarded as an essential step to the formation and development of a vocation and a career. To the lower-class delinquent boy, the school means restraint and compliance. He may not relate the school to a career because he is hazy about his vocational future. His chafing at the discipline of a teacher as another female authority may make the peers of the street a welcome haven. Then his truancy is held accountable by law. He conceals from his family whatever mischief he engages in with his peers; and this becomes intensified by his truancy from school. Such action binds him more closely to his peers who share his deviant views. In addition, youths who lack basic skills in reading and arithmetic may find school subjects overwhelming, while regarding its discipline as oppressive. Thus the truancy rates among delinquents are very high. One study by Bernice

Moore reported that of the delinquent youths she investigated, 95 percent of the 17 year olds, 85 percent of the 16 year olds and 50 percent of the 15 year olds were not attending school, and about 61 percent of the youths between the ages of 15 and 17 were in a truant status or had dropped out of school.[18]

Alienated from his family and school, the youthful delinquent then may depend upon his street associates for direction, as well as for a sense of belonging and acceptance.

Estrangement and Modes of Rationalizations

Although delinquents are estranged from conventional society, they are aware of certain continuities between their way of life and those of conventional society. Since they realize that their behavior is illegal and considered "wrong," they develop rationalizations to justify their activities and to neutralize their illegal actions. First, they may shift the blame for wrongdoing to forces beyond their control such as neglecting parents and a "bad" neighborhood, thereby indirectly denying responsibility for their offenses. Second, they may "deny the victim" by minimizing the injuries or losses inflicted upon him. In stealing a car they are really "borrowing" it. Third, they may claim that the victim deserved his losses or injuries in the context of the occurrence. Fourth, they "condemn the condemners" whom they accuse of spiteful and hypocritical motives. Fifth, they speak of appealing to the higher loyalty to their companions rather than to the laws of a

18. Bernice M. Moore, "The Schools and the Problems of Delinquency: Research and Findings," *Crime and Delinquency* (March, 1961) 7:1:201-212.

vague, conventional, and seemingly hostile society.[19]

Stereotypes of the Victims

In denying the significance of the victim, they also develop stereotypes of their victims. Herman and Julia Schwendinger have pointed out that delinquents further justify their behavior by emphasizing that the means justifies the end. By reversing roles they cast the victims as deviant while they are the morally indignant avengers. Thus the businessman is viewed as a "dishonest merchant" or a "monolithic miser" whom they must oppose. Or the victim may lack respect because he lacks smartness or masculinity and may be called a "punk," "fag," or "chump."[20] Besides these stereotyped versions of the victim, he is necessarily a member of an out-group, a stranger, and automatically legitimate prey for their predatory intentions.

Conflict and Estrangement in the Family

Although the family is the crucial social unit in personality formation and development, the delinquent learns his modes of stealing predominantly from peers, unless he acquires these patterns from the family. His parental influences may mold his basic personality structure; but the modes of conflict contribute to a process of estrangement from the family, and such conflict is reflected in the deviant, restless, aggressive rebellious attitudes of delinquents. As Healy and Bronner, and the Gluecks have pointed out, the fathers, when present, were unable to sustain positive and warm relations with their sons and were in frequent conflict with them.[21]

The delinquents manifested a wide discontinuity between their values and those of their parents. During the first third of this century the generation gap was attributed to the culture gap between foreign-born parents and native-born children. But this gap has persisted into the final third of this century, despite the circumstance of delinquents having native-born parents. This parent-youth intergenerational discontinuity in the midst of a rapidly changing urban context finds one expression in the delinquent's disregard for parental values and his preference for the values of his peers.

Miller has reported that in the lower strata of Boston the one-sex peer relationship is more important than the two-parent family.[22]

Another motivational result of the mother-headed family, is the youth's compensatory drive for masculinity consistent with the focal concern of toughness. Cloward and Ohlin, and Tennyson have stressed, however, that compensatory masculinity as a contributing cause of delinquency has not been definitely verified.[23]

19. Gresham Sykes and David Matza, "Techniques of Neutralization: A Theory of Delinquency," *American Sociological Review* (December, 1947) 22:6:664-670.

20. Herman and Julia Schwendinger, "Delinquent Stereotypes of Probable Victims," *Juvenile Gangs in Context*, ed. Malcolm W. Klein (Englewood Cliffs, N. J.: Prentice-Hall, Inc., 1967) pp. 91-105.

21. Wm. Healy and Augusta Bronner, *New Light on Delinquency and its Treatment* (New Haven: Yale University Press, 1936); Sheldon and Eleanor Glueck, *Unraveling Juvenile Delinquency*.

22. Walter B. Miller, "Implications of Urban Lower Class Culture for Social Work," *Social Science Review* (September, 1955) p. 33.

23. Cloward and Ohlin, *Delinquency and Opportunity*; Ray A. Tennyson, "Family Structure and Delinquent Behavior," *Juvenile Gangs in Context*, ed. Malcolm W. Klein (Englewood Cliffs, N. J.: Prentice-Hall, Inc., 1967) pp. 57-69.

What About Middle Class Delinquency?

One of the oversights in these analyses of delinquent subcultures is the existence of middle class delinquent groups. Seemingly, the studies of self-reported delinquent behavior indicate a prevalence of delinquent behavior among middle class youths who are not caught. But some are caught, and their deviant behavior seems to fit into a definite pattern which contrasts with that of the lower class delinquents. First, they tend to deviate by hedonic activities, such as drinking, drugs, sex escapades, gambling, drag racing, a situation which is not unlike that of the younger deviants whom Cohen described. Second, they are involved in stealing cars for "joy rides," and later they tend to abandon them. Vaz, in his study of 1639 white high school boys from grades 9 through 13, reported that the older youths who resort to these deviant activities which were sanctioned within their 15 to 19 subculture included by percentages: petty theft, "taking little things," 67.2; gambling, 66; vandalism, 52; fighting, 56; tried to be intimate with a member of the opposite sex, 37.8. By contrast, very few youths tried to break and enter, 7.5 percent; and only 1.0 percent tried to use, buy, or sell drugs. Thus, in contrast to middle class youths, the emphasis among arrested delinquents is on serious theft, and these are predominantly from the lower class. Among middle class youths serious theft appears to be infrequent and use of or traffic in drugs, at least in 1963 was also a relatively infrequent practice, as judged by this study.[24]

The middle class youths who were prone to become delinquents included those on the periphery of the educational system, and outside the scope of social acceptance.

SOCIAL FACTORS AND PERSONALITY TRAITS

Residential Distribution of Delinquents

Delinquents concentrate in physically deteriorated and socially disorganized slum areas of the inner city where there are high rates of adult crime, drug addiction, prostitution, alcoholism, unemployment and poverty. In these communities there are high percentages of unskilled and semi-skilled workers, families on welfare, one-parent families, especially mother-headed families.

Before 1930 the disorganized, high-rate delinquency areas were adjacent to the business district or center of the city, while the percentages of delinquency declined with distance from the center of the city. But this pattern of delinquent distribution no longer applies because the growth of the city has changed, some sections have been rebuilt, while deterioration and disorganization have spread to other areas far from the metropolitan center.[25]

Delinquency and Minority Groups

Delinquency rates are high among recently settled immigrant groups. Children of ethnic groups who have recently settled in the urban community become exposed to delinquent values because the areas in which they settle have high rates of delinquency.

Before World War II, the dominant delinquent groups were the children of the

24. Edmund W. Vaz, ed., *Middle Class Juvenile Delinquency* (New York: Harper & Row, Publishers, 1967).

25. Henry D. McKay, "A Note on Trends in Rates of Delinquency in Certain Areas of Chicago," President's Commission of Law Enforcement and Administration of Justice." *Task Force Report: Juvenile Delinquency and Youth Crime* (Washington D. C.: U.S. Government Printing Office, 1967) pp. 114-118.

eastern and southern European immigrants. As these families settled in the urban areas their children acquired negative attitudes and techniques from delinquent residents in the areas, with whom they associated. Thus successively the high rates of delinquency were noted through the years from the beginning of the present century for Scandinavian, German, Irish, Polish, Jewish, Italian, Mexican, Appalachian white, Black, and Puerto Rican residents.[26] Since World War II, with the immigration of the southern whites and racial minorities, these ethnic and racial groups have the highest rates of delinquency. In this sense delinquency is a function of recency of settlement in an urban slum community, and also is influenced by the social class and traditions of the ethnic group.

Ethnic groups who were motivated to acquire occupational skills and education moved away from the slums into middle class areas. Hence the children of these groups did not become or remain delinquents.[27]

Although delinquency may be attributed to race, the fact is that race in itself is not conducive to delinquency. Middle class blacks have relatively low rates of delinquency. The important considerations are the factors of recency of settlement into the urban community, the contact of children with delinquent youths in the area of settlement, together with the background and motivations of the ethnic or racial groups to acquire the training and/or education qualifying them to move away from high rate delinquency areas.

The "Broken Home"

The family "broken" by the death of one or both parents, by parental divorce, or by parental separation, inevitably experiences an interval of family disorganization. One parent has to accept the roles of both, either by working and caring for the home, or the solitary parent has to hire a substitute parent figure to assume the other role. How does the "broken home" contribute to delinquency?

Shaw and McKay found that the ratio for broken homes between nondelinquents was 1.18 to 1 for boys, and 1.49 to 1 for girls, which may indicate that the broken home has a greater influence upon girls than upon boys.[28] Cavan compared the broken and intact homes of delinquents in five different studies. The girl delinquents showed a greater discrepancy than the girl nondelinquents, but the boy delinquents and nondelinquents did not differ so markedly. But, the rates of broken homes for delinquent girls are far higher than for delinquent boys, and the rates for delinquent boys are higher than for those of nondelinquent boys.[29] Although many investigators regard the broken home as a contributing factor in delinquency, its direct or indirect influence upon delinquency must be qualified.

First, the proportion of broken homes among delinquents increases with the age of the delinquents studied. Second, the

26. Bernard Lander, *Understanding Juvenile Delinquency* (Columbia University Press, 1954). Also Shaw and McKay, "Social Factors in Juvenile Delinquency.

27. Cloward and Ohlin, *Delinquency and Opportunity.*

28. Clifford R. Shaw and Henry V. McKay, "Social Factors in Juvenile Delinquency," *Causes of Crime*, National Commission on Law Observance and Enforcement 1312 (Washington D. C.: U.S. Government Printing Office, 1931) pp. 281-284.

29. Ruth Cavan, *Juvenile Delinquency*, pp. 184-187.

child from a broken home is more likely to be committed to an institution than a child from a complete home, because officials may consider that the broken home is a basis for commitment. Third, the frequency of broken homes varies by type of delinquency. A higher proportion of incorrigible children and truants come from broken homes than do property offenders, traffic violators, and those charged with misdemeanors.

Fourth, the rates of broken homes vary by ethnic group. Of Negro delinquents, 66.0 percent, of Italians, 27.4 percent; and of the American delinquents, 40 percent, came from broken homes.[30]

Fifth, the broken home tends to have a more perceptible influence upon the female than upon the male delinquents; and significantly more delinquent girls than delinquent boys come from broken homes.

Sixth, the families which become disrupted by the death of one or both parents do not tend to affect the juveniles in the same way as families which become disrupted by desertion or divorce. The bereaved family members may draw closer together, while family members disturbed by parental conflict may have divided loyalties.

Personality Traits and Delinquency

What part does personality play in the onset of delinquency? Many clinicians have insisted that delinquency results from personality traits such as low intelligence and emotional instability. Before World War I, many criminologists believed delinquency resulted from mental deficiency. This hypothesis was discredited in part when the army recruits in World War I were tested and their intelligence scores were found to be relatively lower than was expected.

Mentally defective persons do not have higher rates of delinquency than youths in comparable socioeconomic situations. Seemingly, they may be exploited by other delinquents and are more apt to be caught than delinquents of normal or above intelligence. Also they are usually rejected by delinquents for the more complex types of theft. Although the intelligence of the average delinquent is about dull normal, this intelligence level may be a result of defective learning, which in turn is a function of the educational process by the social class.

Are delinquents more disturbed emotionally than nondelinquents? Sociologists contend that by the very process of acceptance by their peer associates they demonstrate a "normality" for social participation. Their delinquency, then, is a subcultural function of the influence of their peers, rather than an expression of an emotionally disturbed personality.[31]

DISPOSITION, CARE, TREATMENT

Disposition and Treatment

The treatment of the delinquent is difficult because of the ambivalent attitudes toward him. He is viewed as a predator and a menace from whom the community must be protected, but on the other hand he is considered a youth in distress, (unlike an adult), and one who must be helped

---

30. Shaw and McKay, "Social Factors."

31. See Stark Hathaway and Eli D. Monachesi, *Analyzing and Predicting Juvenile Delinquency With the MMPI* (Minneapolis: University of Minnesota Press, 1953).

by the court to become adapted to the community. Ideologically, the juvenile court was designed to help the underage person as a child whose needs and problems must be determined, in order to facilitate the child's rehabilitation. Thus the youngster theoretically was judged in terms of his needs rather than in terms of his offense. But these high-minded principles were not always observed, because no matter what the juvenile court claimed, it turned out frequently that the juvenile accused of committing an offense lacked legal counsel to prove he might not have committed the offense. And if he did not commit the crime or misdemeanor, he might not want the juvenile court's help, and certainly would oppose having a court record. Also, the court's assertions about wanting to help were not substantiated by the type of institution to which the delinquent was sent. Often this resembled a prison. As a reaction, certain improvements have been made. The juvenile as one accountable to law by truancy is differentiated from the juvenile who is charged with a felony. But in addition, the young person, whatever his charge, has the right to counsel, whether or not he can afford it.

Control: Rehabilitation and Prevention

How can delinquency be controlled and its scope reduced? The approach to such control depends upon one's view of the causes of delinquency. If this phenomena is viewed as a mental health problem, with its causes inherent in personality problems of the offender, then the appropriate sequence of action would be to treat the offender at a mental health clinic. The difficulty with this individualistic approach is that many delinquents are not necessarily

emotionally disturbed, even as some non-delinquents are emotionally disturbed. Also, some delinquents who are thus disturbed do not necessarily deviate because of their emotional difficulties, but rather because of pressure by delinquent associates. Thus even if delinquents were treated for their mental health they might still persist in their predatory behavior.

Since delinquency as manifested in stealing and other group offenses is learned in the streets and at times in the home, to offset this deviancy, the delinquent's orientations and his neighborhood and peer influences must be changed. In as much as the purpose of rehabilitation is to reorient the delinquent to a law-abiding way of life, the neighborhood, including the delinquent gangs, would have to be controlled to minimize their adverse social influence upon the youth.

Two broad approaches for changing the delinquent include 1) the intramural efforts within the correctional institution, and 2) extramural influences within the community.

Correctional Institutions and Training Schools

Correctional institutions ostensibly strive to reorient the delinquent through formal education and vocational training, and if possible, by identification with conventional role-models and groups. However, most correctional institutions and training schools are chiefly concerned with enforcing discipline, preventing escapes, and using the labor of the inmates to maintain the institution. In addition, they usually provide formal education and rudimentary occupational training. Thus the confinement, restraints and the forced assignments give the inmates the impression that they are within the bounds of a modified prison.

Their preoccupation with institutional maintenance and custodial functions diverts the attention of the staff from rehabilitation. Such rehabilitation, too, varies in degree and scope. Some inmates can complete their elementary or high school education; others can learn the fundamentals of vocational skills, such as auto mechanics or welding. The difficulty with vocational training is that it lacks continuity with employment outside the institution.

Although many correctional and training institutions have a clinical staff composed of a psychiatrist, psychologist, and social workers, such personnel in themselves do not necessarily assure the success of a rehabilitation program. First, the youths who associate the clinical with the administrative staff suspect them of betraying confidences revealed for therapeutic purposes. The youths might hesitate or even refuse to disclose personal problems to the clinical staff. Some boys who seek counsel may be suspected of being administrative stooges. Unless the inmates cooperate with the clinical staff it is doubtful that any concerted psychotherapy could be implemented. As a consequence, individual and group therapy are usually not effective in these institutions.

Zald and Street studied four youth institutions from the viewpoint of organization, inmate response, and staff-inmate relations. They selected two custodial-oriented institutions; here the boys were discouraged from making friends, encouraged to keep to themselves, and in general induced to conform. In treatment-oriented institutions, the boys were encouraged to cultivate friends and to be friendly with the staff. Although the boys in the treatment-oriented

institution gave the staff more trouble, they were less hostile to the staff and to the institution than the boys in the custodial institution.[32]

Generally, the correctional facility is custodial in emphasis so that the rehabilitative functions are reduced and subordinated to maintaining discipline. As a result, the present trend is toward seeking to change the milder offenders through controlled guidance in the community.

Efforts at Prevention

For prevention purposes, the local community must be encouraged to provide the type of institutions and groups which may deter the juveniles from becoming delinquents. The unit of organization is the local community. Such activity involves the cooperation and services of leaders, businessmen, school officials and teachers, police, welfare agencies, the settlement house, and the clinics to help the members of the community. In addition, trained prevention-workers are employed to work with delinquent boys' gangs. One prevention project in this category and with this orientation is the Chicago Area Project.

The Chicago Area Project has as its point of departure the local community, which is the unit for delinquency prevention. Within the urban subdivision or barro, the local residents are organized, and from their ranks whom the indigenous "natural leaders" are selected. The juvenile worker strives to reorient the boys' gangs by fostering greater interaction between delinquent and law-abiding persons, and by involving them in constructive acts within the community.

32. Mayer N. Zald and David Street, "Custody and Treatment in Juvenile Institutions," *Crime and Delinquency* (July, 1964) 10:249-256.

One of the serious difficulties in the prevention programs for delinquents is the lack of economic resources and opportunities for the youths and their families. A boy or youth cannot effectively change his attitudes about stealing when he believes that he must forcibly remain idle. He feels that somehow the institutions of society are failing in their functions, that the leaders are indifferent to his fate. Thus economic opportunities must be integrated in a prevention or rehabilitation program.

The Task Force Report by the President's commission has recognized this fact and recommended the following changes to facilitate prevention of delinquency: 1) the reduction of unemployment among youth, 2) a minimum family income, 3) a welfare policy to keep the family together, 4) improvement of housing and recreation facilities, and 5) help in problems of domestic management and child care. In addition, youth gangs must be reoriented.

For Further Reading

Cloward, Richard A. and Ohlin, Lloyd E. *Delinquency and Opportunity*. New York: The Free Press, 1960.

This volume analyzes the neighborhood conditions and personality needs of three types of delinquent behavior.

Giallombardo, Rose, ed. *Juvenile Delinquency: A Book of Readings*. New York: John Wiley & Sons, Inc., 1966.

An excellent series of articles dealing with the contributing causes to delinquency and the efforts at treatment and control.

Glueck, Sheldon and Eleanor. *Unraveling Juvenile Delinquency*. Cambridge, Massachusetts: Harvard University Press, 1950.

A comparative analysis of matched groups of 550 delinquents and 500 nondelinquents in order to determine what family and personality conditions contribute directly to delinquent behavior among males.

Short, James F. and Strodtbeck, Fred L. *Group Process and Delinquency*. Chicago: University of Chicago Press, 1965.

An intensive analysis of the effects of peer relations upon delinquent behavior as well as a study of delinquent subculture.

3 | Drug Use and Opiate Addiction

DRUGS are used so pervasively in society that we have been called a "drug culture." Drugs, which are extremely beneficial as well as harmful, can alleviate pain, reduce tension, contribute to the recovery of the mentally ill, induce euphoria and commit the user to a binding addiction. Many drugs which are sold over the counter help relieve the discomforts or sufferings of millions of people. Other drugs are bought by the sick only by prescription for specified medicinal purposes, and some drugs which are illegitimate are sold in the black market and used mainly for euphoria or "kicks," with addictive effects.[1] In this chapter, I deal with illicit drugs, the users of which are defined as deviants. Heroin is the chief object of our analysis, but marihuana (marijuana) also is considered in terms of its function in deviant behavior. The following aspects of deviant drug use are discussed: (1) the differences between heroin, marihuana, and other selected drugs, (2) the extent of heroin and marihuana use in contemporary society, (3) the social processes, factors and personality traits affecting opiate addicts, and (4) the control of addiction by the treatment and prevention of addiction, and by the suppression of illegal drug traffic.

HEROIN, MARIHUANA AND OTHER DRUGS

Heroin as a narcotic evokes emotion-laden images of addiction, mind-expansion, and violence. Narcotics include opiates consisting of opium, morphine, heroin, and codeine, and opium-like synthetic drugs, covering demoral, the brand-name for mepredine-hypochloride, and methadone. Heroin is the chief villain among the opiates. It may relieve physical pain, mental anguish, induce sleep and stupor, as well as stimulate euphoria; but it enslaves the user in a binding addiction.

Marihuana is not a narcotic and is not addictive. Its effects differ completely from those of opiates. Its enjoyment varies with the smoker's disposition. It induces a greater sense of body awareness and a euphoria which suffuses through the organism. It does not make the smoker violent, but induces a sense of mirth that leads to hilarity. The smoker's desire to speak and to concentrate may diminish. Marihuana is made from the leaves of the hemp plant (*cannabis sativa* or *cannabis indica*), which also produces a fiber for making ropes. Despite

1. Robert Coles, Joseph H. Brenner, and Dermot Meagher, *Drugs and Youth* (New York: Liveright, 1970).

30

the publicity about the dangers of marihuana and the penalties for its possession or use, it is not more harmful than alcohol. But its illegality, apparently based upon misinformation concerning its properties, involves a penalty.[2] As more research on this drug is reported, the penalties for the use of marihuana have become lighter. Nonetheless, its status as an illegal substance affects the user, when he is apprehended. It can cause embarrassment, discomfort and stigma resulting from trial and disposition, which frequently is probation.

Cocaine, which is estimated in one survey to have been tried at least once by four million people, has the effects of a stimulant. Usually sniffed, it induces an euphoria as well as a greater stimulation to the user,—more than the other drugs mentioned.

Amphetamines are widely used among the youth and by some adults for the intrinsic stimulation effects and to avert depression.

LSD (Lyseric Acid) has been used mainly by middle-class students because of its supposed "mind-expanding" effects; this also means that the individual user may lose his sense of self-boundaries with probable impulsive hallucinatory effects.[3]

EXTENT OF OPIATE ADDICTION AND DRUG USE

Since World War II heroin addiction in the United States has been characterized as an epidemic. Its spread has afflicted mainly lower class youth among the racial

2. David P. Ausubel, *Drug Addiction* (New York: Random House, Inc., 1966), pp. 95, 96.
3. Joseph Newman (director), *What Everyone Needs to Know About Drugs* (Washington, D. C.: U.S. News and World Report Inc., 1970), A Young Woman Tells Her Story—Chapter 10. pp. 130, 131.

Table 3.1

Types of Drugs, Their Slang Names, Their Uses and Effects

Name	Slang Name	How Taken	Duration	Classification	Long-Term Effects
HEROIN	H, horse, scag, smack, junk, dope.	Injected or Sniffed	4 Hours	Narcotic	Total addiction, withdrawal pains, moral and physical deterioration.
COCAINE	Coke, snow, gold dust, star dust.	Sniffed, Swallowed or Injected	Varies, Short	Stimulant Local Anesthesia	Deterioration of nasal passages, damage to blood vessels.
MARIJUANA	Pot, grass, smoke, tea, dope, hashish, hash, reefers.	Smoked, Swallowed or Sniffed	4 Hours	Relaxant, Euphoriant	?
BARBITURATES	Christmas trees, trees, reds, yellow jackets, yellows, blues, blue birds, blue heavens.	Swallowed or Injected	4 Hours	Sedative-Hypnotic	Addiction with severe withdrawal pains, possible convulsions, toxic psychosis, deterioration of body organs.
AMPHETAMINES	Speed, dexies, hearts, footballs, pep pills, co-pilots, roses, purple hearts.	Swallowed or Injected	4 Hours	Sympatho-Mimetic	Loss of appetite, delusions, hallucinations, toxic psychosis, deterioration of body organs.
LSD	Acid, sugar, D, L, Big D, pearly gates, purple haze.	Swallowed	10 Hours	Hallucinogen	May intensify existing psychosis, panic reaction, recurrence of hallucinations.
METHAQUALONE	Sopors, love drug, love pill, Quads.	Swallowed	4 Hours	Nonbarbiturate Sedative-Hypnotic	Apparent addiction, severe withdrawal pains, possible lethal overdose.
THC	None	Smoked, Swallowed or Sniffed	4-10 Hours	Stimulant, Depressant or Hallucinogen	Nonaddictive, fatigue, psychosis.
SERNYL	PCP, peace pill.	Smoked or Swallowed	10-12 Hours	Tranquilizer with Hallucinogenic Properties	Possible addiction with extended use.

minorities, in the large metropolitan centers. But it has also affected middle- and upper middle-class youth and adults. It has "hooked" women as well as men, black and white, and persons of almost all ages. Over two million persons admit to have taken heroin at least once, with an estimated 400,000 addicts.

In 1969, 68,088 cases of opiate addiction represented the cases on file in the varied agencies which reported their figures to the Bureau of Narcotics and Dangerous Drugs. But this number cannot be accurate, because an estimated 100,000 opiate addicts reside in New York City alone.[4] The estimate of 400,000 opiate addicts indicates an increase so marked over the estimated 60,000 addicts in 1960 as to be considered a social problem of crisis proportions. Fortunately, this wide-spread use of heroin is believed to have reached a peak and to be declining in appeal and use; and this has become a staunch hope. For example, one survey of Chicago and suburban high schools by a team of reporters who interviewed hundreds of school officials, teachers, parents, and social workers, reported that while marihuana was as accessible as tobacco, heroin though available, was rarely used. The use of LSD had declined or had stabilized in demand, but the use of alcohol increased dramatically.[5] Other factors which indicated the levelling off of heroin use are the decline of deaths attributed to drug overdose, and of arrests for drug use.

CHANGED POLICY AND TREATMENT OF OPIATE USERS

Before 1914 an opiate could be bought legally over the drug counter. But the Harrison Narcotic Act of 1914 and subsequent amendments restricted the imports, sale, and manufacture of opium and its derivatives. It permitted licensed dealers to dispense opiates for medicinal purposes only. This law required the retention of records of these transactions; it made the possession and use of narcotics a crime, and doctors were admonished to prescribe the opiates only for genuine medical needs and not to satisfy the cravings of the addicted. Since at least 100,000 addicts were cut off from the opiates and treatment facilities were unavailable, the suffering among this group was intense.[6]

New York and other large cities opened ambulatory clinics to rehabilitate and protect addicts from becoming victimized by criminals who were then beginning to exploit a black market in opiates. By 1919, however, officials campaigned for a more punitive policy against addicts and drug traffickers. Their agitation was effective. The hue and cry in press and public was hostile to addicts. By 1923 clinics were closed, and addicts were depicted as moral degenerates and criminals rather than as victims of distressing and uncontrollable cravings for the opiate.[7]

HEROIN USE AS A PERSONAL-SOCIAL REACTION

Unless a person has an allergy to heroin, he is prone to becoming addicted. This addiction arises because of the addictive effects of the drug. When deprived of the opiate distress symptoms arise. After about 8 hours, the user becomes tense, restless and

4. Alfred Lindesmith, *Addiction and Opiates* (Aldine-Atherton, Inc., 1968).

5. *Chicago Sun Times.*

6. Alfred Lindesmith, *The Addict and the Law* (Bloomington, Indiana: Indiana University Press, 1965) pp. 21-25.

7. *Ibid.*

has difficulty sleeping. After sixteen hours, he becomes more restless and tense. He sweats, yawns, and experiences diarrhea. Within twenty-four hours, his skin reveals gooseflesh. He experiences hot flashes, cramps in his legs and arms, and nausea. After about 72 hours his distressing withdrawal symptoms begin to recede in intensity. But the addict does not wait that long. Since the heroin not only quiets his distressing symptoms but also creates an euphoric condition, he acquires an insatiable craving for the opiate, which drives him to extreme measures to acquire funds to buy the heroin.[8]

But these distress symptoms do not inevitably lead to an addiction, unless the person realizes that the opiate can quiet these symptoms. Suppose an injured or sick person is hospitalized. He is administered a substance to help him sleep or ease his pain, but he does not know what the substance is. As he improves and is discharged from the hospital, he may experience withdrawal symptoms which he regards as the lingering effects of his injury or illness. He may take aspirin or some other legitimate drug to ease his pain; in several days his discomfort will abate and hence he will have escaped addiction.

Addiction, then, seemingly arises when the user can relate the withdrawal symptoms to deprivation of the drug and realize that the drug also quiets the withdrawal distress. This realization of the drug's relations to his symptoms as well as to inducing a certain euphoria, makes him "hooked" to the drug. Being "hooked" is a self-definition of a social craving, and the interpretation is usually communicated by his street associates, who frequently are addicts themselves.[9]

Without funds, the male addict is forced to steal, mug, rob, hustle, while the female may resort to shoplifting or prostitution. The heroin addict is defined, and defines himself, as a user—a deviant—and differentiates himself from nonusers. He realizes his basic addiction when he strives to stop but cannot and when he must persist in getting funds for the drug. As a self-defined addict, he must resort to criminal behavior, whether by theft or mugging to "get the bread" to pay the pusher. He necessarily becomes involved in an illegitimate network of persons to "fence" his stolen merchandise, to provide his pusher, and he must devise ways of evading the police and the hidden agent seeking to detect him.[10]

DRUG ADDICTION IS LEARNED AS A SOCIAL EXPERIENCE

Although the spread of addiction among youth is sometimes attributed to sinister figures from organized crime and the Mafia, studies have reported that peers tend to influence each other to take the opiate and to share the "high." Hughes and Jaffe studied several communities where outbreaks of drug addiction occurred among over fifty addicts, a situation which they called "macroepidemics." They found that the epidemics developed among close friends.[11]

But the acquisition of drug addiction among isolated drug users frequently was

8. David P. Ausubel, *Drug Addiction*.

9. Alfred Lindesmith, *Addiction and Opiates*; and Yves J. Kron and Edward M. Brown, *Mainline to Nowhere: The Making of a Heroin Addict* (New York: World Publishing Company, 1967).

10. Isidor Chein, "Narcotics Use Among Juveniles," *Social Work* (April, 1956), 1:2:50-60; Edwin M. Schur, *Crimes Without Victims* (Englewood Cliffs, N. J.: Prentice-Hall, Inc., 1965) pp. 122-128.

11. Patrick H. Hughes and Jerome H. Jaffe, "Heroin Epidemics in Chicago," *Paper presented at the World Congress of Psychiatry* (November 28, 1971), Mexico City.

transmitted by a sibling or a spouse who as a heroin user also tended to be isolated. One female addict admitted that she acquired the habit from her boyfriend who said to her:[12]

> It's good. Use it and you'll find out how good it is. You'll feel so good, Carmen, use it, go ahead. I'll show you how to use it."

Her withdrawal distress and craving for a "high" forced her to rob, steal, and mug. As a junkie she accepted prostitution as the easiest way to pay the high cost of her drugs.

Although some initial users of opiates are still experimenting and somehow have not been addicted and committed, those who are addicted and define themselves as users, tend to seek out other addicts and seem to avoid nonusers. Some addicts tend to proselytize others in order to have companionship in the use of the opiate. Thus, they seek out their friends and try to induce them to try the drug, as has been pointed out. In this respect, drug addiction becomes a communicable practice and spreads by primary relations among peers in given areas, although this contagion may also leap into other areas. Because of the central focus of the opiate in their way of life, the development of a special argot and among some addicts a particular kind of handclasp, they tend to become an in-group with a distinct contra-culture.

DRUG SUBCULTURES IN THE SOCIETAL CONTEXT

The drug culture that characterizes contemporary society represents one reaction to competitiveness and mind-presence of urbanism-industrialism and the need to escape from its rigors. However, this escape has assumed a more concerted direction among youth and adults, who have become "turned on" by drugs, which constitute a symbol of defiance and rebellion against this form of utilitarianism. The terms "beatniks," "acid-heads," "swingers," "hippies," "pot," and "drop-outs," represent a lexicon of counter-competition and utility. Those who failed in the competitive process mingled with those who renounced competition and left its routinized uniformity. A series of deviant subcultures arose. The beatniks emphasized the "creative" experience. The "psychedelics," by their mind-expansion drugs, felt they could experience an individuality of each "doing his own thing." From the lower stratum and especially among the blacks, another subculture emerged which culminated in the social type, the "cool cat" who could resist the 9 to 5 regimen of the working "square." Usually an unskilled youth in the lower stratum, marginal to the mainstream of a competitive working society, he felt justified in preying upon it to fulfill his sensate drug habit. Thus, the middle class drug user announced, by using LSD, his aversion to "growing up absurd" by an adulthood which would be the consequence of conforming uncritically to the utility of a job. The lower-class drug user denounced a society in which he could not participate economically except in the most menial jobs. Thus, he would not be victimized by its routine, but live off this society for his own sensate gratification through the drug. This consensus of nonparticipation was reflected further in the "drop-outs" and the commune dwellers who left the mainstream of society to live as they pleased.[13]

12. Jeremy Larner and Ralph Teffertetler, *The Addict in the Street* (New York: Grove Press, Inc., 1964) pp. 120-145.

13. See Alvin W. Gouldner, *The Coming Crisis of Western Sociology* (New York: Basic Books, Inc., Publishers, 1970) pp. 76-81.

The traditional institutions and norms, whether in marriage or individualism, were subordinate to a collective fulfillment. This general trend has been caricatured as a kind of "romanticism" straying from the compulsory realism impelled by a methodical, "presence of mind" society. But in its accent upon the nonroutine, the sensate, the "creative," the individually different, however, often rationalizations of mediocrity, the encouragement of individual expression was apparent, even though it was channeled into mass form and assumed a new uniformity. While the opiate addict is involved in behavior which is consistent with a rebellious orientation, he also is involved in illegal acts. The subculture among opiate addicts includes the specifics of participating in an illegal black market as well as obtaining the funds, and injecting the drug.

OPIATE ADDICTION AND MARIHUANA IN THE CONTRA-CULTURE

The opiate contra-culture is manifest in the addicts' argot or jargon, their techniques and knowledge about drugs, their network of relations in obtaining access to the drugs, their "hangouts," as well as their defenses against detection and arrest by the police. Opiate addiction becomes a way of life shared by other addicts. It is a counter-culture, because the acquisition, possession and use of drugs are illegal, and its users are opposed to the larger culture.

Within the youth drug slum culture in many large cities, the heroin "kick" is recognized as the supreme "kick," the "horse." The youth may shift from marihuana or other drugs to heroin within this culture, to get a "stronger kick"; but this sequence while peculiar to some youths, does not imply a pharmacological or psychobiolog-

ical relationship between the two types of drugs or any inevitable social sequence in their use.[14]

Among Black drug addicts in this contra-culture, the one definable social type is the "cat" as contrasted with the "gorilla." The cat strives to "hustle" for money in a non-violent way in contrast to the gorilla, who resorts to force. The "cat" aspires "to live without working," but by persuasion and outsmarting others. He operates in a milieu of dishonesty and deception. The "cat" tends to know the drug culture. In getting money for his drugs he knows how to deal with "pushers" and how much junk to inject into his system.

The dominant feature of this "cat" culture is the pursuit of the "kick," the thrill, the "high." From this vantage point, every "cat" has a "kick," whether alcohol, marihuana, addicting drugs, sex, hot or cool jazz, in combination or singly. The drug addicted "cat" acquires a certain "hustle" or impatient acceleration, a state in which he believes in manipulating and "conning" accessible[15] persons to acquire funds for his drugs. In rationalizing his superiority to the "squares" of conventional society, he assumes a calm, serene manner, cultivates a discriminating vocabulary and ritualized gestures by which he manifests his sense of difference from conventional "squares."

DRUGS AS A PROCESS OF ESTRANGEMENT

The use of drugs, especially heroin, is a way of estrangement from conventional values and participation. Ohlin and Cloward

14. Isidor Chein, et al., *The Road to "H": Narcotics, Delinquency and Social Policy* (New York: Basic Books Inc., Publishers, 1964).
15. Harold Finestone, "Cats, Kicks and Color," *Social Problems* (July, 1957) 5:1:3-13.

who applied the theories of Merton to the delinquent subculture; the delinquents who used drugs had not succeeded in their conventional aspirations and also were rejected by criminal groups. Ohlin and Cloward have indicated:[16]

Subcultural drug users in lower-class areas perceive themselves as culturally and socially detached from the life-style and everyday preoccupations of members of the conventional world.

But this withdrawal is an escape, not only from the competitive mainstream of life, but also from interpersonal rejection.[17]

The addict's estrangement from conventional society can be traced with a measure of consistency to his rebellious attitude toward his parents amid the interpersonal strains within the family. Chein reported that compared with nonusers, the addicts were in families in which 97 percent reported disturbed marital as well as family relations. This included the separation and divorce of the parents as well as persistent quarrelling and a general lack of warmth among the family members. The singular theme experienced by male youths was the lack of a warm relationship with their fathers. Thus, the addict's alienation had its psychological roots in the estrangement from the father and from the family.[18] In itself, while plausible, it must be kept in mind that father-son strain occurs among many lower class families, whether or not any pathology eventually ensues. Thus, the estrangement in the family, while consistent with later revolt against establishment ethics, required the influence of street associates and later contacts for its rebellious channelling. This acquisition of a "hang-loose" ethic meant that they opposed the routine, the values, the rigorous, competitive life of the establishment. Their

failure in or renunciation of the school and work world reinforced their rebellious orientation and predisposed their withdrawal from this mainstream of social reality.[19]

Since World War II, the most conspicuous change that has emerged among opiate addicts is the increasing proportion of lower-class youths who have become addicted. Slum dwellers, poverty-ridden, they are least able to pay for the exorbitant price of the opiates. Prior to World War II, very few youths were addicts. Of 2,349 cases investigated in one study, only twelve, half of one percent were under 20 and over 90 percent were older than 25.[20]

In 1951, a survey of opiate addicts in Chicago indicated changes, because about half were under 26 years old. Among hospitalized patients at Lexington, Kentucky, it was reported that in 1940, 5.2 percent were age 25 or younger. In 1950 about 32 percent were younger than age 25 and in 1964 about 27 percent were under 25. Thus, it is evident that a sharp rise in the percentage of youthful addicts occured after World War II, and remained relatively high.

Over 80 percent of the Chicago addicts were males. Approximately three out of four

---

16. Richard A. Cloward and Lloyd E. Chlin, *Delinquency and Opportunity* (New York: The Free Press, 1960); See also D. M. Wilmer, et al., "Heroin Use and Street Gangs," *Journal of Criminal Law, Criminology and Police Science* (November-December, 1957) 48:4:399-409.

17. Joseph Newman, directing editor, *What Everyone Needs to Know About Drugs*, (Washington, D. C.: U.S. News and World Report Inc., 1970) pp. 130, 131.

18. Isidor Chein, *The Road to "H."*

19. Alfred Lindesmith and John Gagnon, "Anomie and Drug Addiction," *Anomie and Deviant Behavior*, ed. Marshall B. Clinard (New York: The Free Press, 1964) pp. 174-185.

20. Bingham Dai, *Opium Addiction in Chicago* (Shanghai, China: The Commercial Press Ltd., 1937) pp. 47-48.

lived in slum areas, while the highest rates of delinquency and of adult crime prevailed where residents were in the lowest socio-economic category. Many addicts also were delinquents who participated in youth contra-cultures within these areas.[21]

In 1963, it was evident that the Blacks comprised a very high proportion of addicts, much larger than their proportion in the general population. Of the 48,535 active narcotic addicts, the Blacks comprised 53.9 percent of the total estimated addict population, but constitute only 11 percent of the general population. Among the whites, the Puerto Ricans comprised 11.7 percent, the Mexicans 6.6 percent and the remaining whites, 26.9 percent. All other addicts consisted of 0.9 of one percent.[22]

Personality Traits

Before the heroin epidemic, many researchers emphasized that opiate addicts were essentially unstable and that their opiate addiction resulted from their personality condition. Their reluctance to face responsibilities induced them to escape into drug usage. One prevalent view was that "addict-prone" people become addicted. Kolb reported that of 225 addicts, 85 percent were unstable.[23] This finding is consistent with the clinical view that opiate addiction is the expression of an acting-out disorder, such as psychopathy. Ausubel, with this clinical approach, places them in a kind of omnibus and subjective category when he states that impressive evidence characterizes the majority of drug addicts as "inadequate personalities." Among young addicts the average picture is that of a youth who lacks motivation in school or at work, who is frustrated and anxious, unable to concentrate and passive and de-

pendent.[24] Frequently, these are the characteristics of the frustrations in the slum areas where the institutional outlets are so meager as to inhibit motivation, to affect frustration, and to arouse anxiety. Thus, the tendency to characterize a person removed from the context of life situation of the slums is to depict an abstraction. Nonetheless, it may be argued that in the mainstream of society perhaps the middle and upper middle class outlook and motivation sustain these values. Thus, the individuals who are not motivated by these competitive values of the establishment, who rebel or withdraw, have personalities that reflect the value systems that they incorporate. Other criteria besides the clinical components may indicate their lack of motivation for success. Many failed in their conventional as well as criminal aspirations. In a *selective process*, they appear less stable or at least less competent than those in similar competitive situations. They come from stress-ridden families who would have a depressing or frustrating effect on their personal orientations. They select drug addicts as friends who influence them to become addicted.

With the wide-spread incidence of addiction, the factor of personality became subsidiary to social influences which contrib-

21. Solomon Kobrin, *Drug Addiction Among Young Persons in Chicago* (Chicago: Institute for Juvenile Research, 1953) pp. 61-68.

22. Permanent Subcommittee on Investigations of the Committee on Government Operations, U.S. Senate *Organized Crime and Illicit Traffic in Narcotics,* 1st and 2nd Sessions (Washington D. C.: U.S. Government Printing Office, 1964).

23. Lawrence Kolb, "Types and Characteristics of Drug Addicts," *Mental Hygiene* (July, 1925) 9:3:301-304.

24. David Ausubel, *Drug Addiction*, pp. 42-44. See also Bingham Dai, *Opium Addiction in Chicago.*

uted to drug addiction, such as the local area of residence, the socio-economic status of the family, and the ethnic or racial identity. Within this framework of social factors, personality characteristics may have exerted some influence, but the important consideration is that social factors were more influential than personality instability.

Apparently, access to drugs has a greater influence over the categories of persons who become addicted than does their personal stability. In England before World War II, an estimated 25 percent of the opiate addicts were doctors and nurses, who evidently had access to morphine in the discharge of their medical duties.[25]

But heroin addicts may incorrectly impress others with respect to their personal stability, for two reasons based upon their addiction. First, they will resort to cheating, deception, stealing, and aggression, including robbery and assault, in order to accumulate money for the drug. Second, they manifest intense disorganization under the influence of withdrawal distress, by cursing, irritability, and general instability. To unknowing strangers they would appear as "dope fiends." In addition, the stereotype tends to provide an image of their instability. In their avid pursuit of the opiate, they neglect their appearance, and as one phrased it, "look like bums." In addition, should they seek out a rehabilitation center, they will be considered psychiatric patients.[26]

DRUG ADDICTION AS A SOCIAL PROBLEM

The social consequences of drug addiction ramify so as to affect the very safety of the citizens on the street. Drug addicts cannot defray the costs for their high-priced black market drugs by legitimate employ-

ment. Hence they must steal and prey upon innocent victims to pay for their habit. They may shoplift from stores, a fact which necessitates more mechanical and personal vigilance by storeowners to protect their merchandise. They assault and rob people on the street, so that venturing out after dark becomes hazardous. They burglarize homes, so that law-abiding citizens feel insecure even within the confines of their abodes. Single women who live alone, and aged persons, are especially vulnerable targets for addicts. The social climate of a community changes when drug addicts abound, because they prey upon law-abiding citizens in order to get funds to pay for the opiate.

An estimated $2.8 billion is the value of the property stolen, while $1.1 billion is lost in terms of potential production. Over $800 million is spent in the treatment and prevention of drug addiction, and in the suppression of the drug traffic.

In addition, hundreds of youths die annually from accidental overdoses of drugs.

CONTROL, CARE, TREATMENT, AND PREVENTION

Since the societal reaction depends upon the image of the addict, the revised image of the addict is that instead of a criminal or a "fiend," he is regarded as a patient. Consequently, the approach to the addict has changed largely from punishment to treatment.

25. Edwin M. Schur, *Narcotic Addiction in Britain and America* (Bloomington, Indiana: Indiana University Press, 1956).
26. See S. Kirson Weinberg, *Social Problems in Modern Urban Society* (Englewood Cliffs, N. J.: Prentice-Hall, Inc., 1970) Chapter 16.

Control

Based on contemporary treatment of the addict, he is viewed as patient and as a law violator. The amalgam of this conception is expressed by treating the addict within a penal institution. Sometimes, this combination is forced upon society because the addict violates the law, or may also be a "pusher." Thus he is incarcerated for his use of drugs, but treated as a patient for his addiction. Within the state penal systems, the modes of treatment, however, are not necessarily successful. The diligence and competence of trained personnel to reorient addicts are lacking. Thus most addicts tend to relapse soon after discharge.

On the Federal level, two large hospitals have been devoted exclusively to opiate addicts, at Lexington, Kentucky and Fort Worth, Texas. Maurer and Vogel, who studied the addicted patients, reported that 64 percent were first admissions and 36 percent were readmissions. Among the discharged patients, about 50 percent could not be traced, while 50 percent of those who could be traced abstained. Of those who could not be traced, it seems that many abstained because they would have incurred police records through their infractions.

Federal programs were developed prior to the critical epidemic of this form of addiction. Hospitalization is only one recourse for dealing with this acute and serious problem. Explicitly, what constitutes "cure" as the goal of treatment? "Cure" cannot be considered mere abstinence from the drug at the time of discharge from the hospital only. Abstinence must persist in the unsupervised outside community, amidst the frustrations of daily life.

The "English" System

The "English" system refers to "heroin maintenance" by the government. In England, the opiate addict registers with the government and is allotted an amount of heroin by prescription. This system removes the addict from the criminal underworld as a source of supply. It also dispenses with the need for the addict to steal or mug, and averts prostitution for females. It removes the stigma of addiction which may result in one's becoming a criminal and thief.[27]

This system is somewhat successful in England, but that nation had under 1,000 known addicts who registered, in a nation of 50 million. Later the number of addicts may have risen to over 3,000 in a nation of 55 million. By contrast, opiate addiction in the United States involves over 400,000 persons in a diversified nation of more than 200 million persons. This nation is heterogeneous; England, by comparison, is not. This nation has a history of violence stemming from the frontier and beyond, while England does not. Even the police do not carry firearms. In the United States, recourse to heroin maintenance is viewed as approving and encouraging a diabolical practice. Here also, the addict is younger on the average, tends to be a "street addict" from the slums and hence prone to violence. In England, despite the upsurge of addiction among youths, many addicts are doctors and nurses who have had access to the drug.[28]

27. *U.S. News and World Report* (September 11, 1972).

28. Edwin Schur, *Narcotic Addiction in Britain and America* (Bloomington, Indiana: Indiana University Press, 1956).

Treatment of Drug Addiction

The objective of treatment is to rehabilitate the drug addict by having him abstain from the drug, and by so changing his goals, to enable him to have a productive, self-supporting role in society.

Psychotherapeutic efforts to help opiate addicts achieve abstinence have not been notably successful. In fact, the imprisonment of the drug addict and removing him from access to the opiate does not necessarily lead to sustained abstinence after discharge. Even group therapy achieves varying degrees of abstinence after discharge from a treatment program. One addict, though not necessarily typical, claimed that group therapy resulted in his becoming more hostile to his parents, but did not diminish his binding craving for heroin. His first objective after discharge from prison was to get the opiate. Other addicts hold out longer and some vigorously strive to abstain because of the suffering and humiliation they have endured. But a binding craving, coupled with the frustrations and pressures in their home environment, complicated by street influences, contributed to their relapse.

Methadone Maintenance

As a compromise, methadone, which is a synthetic narcotic without the "high," but which can quiet withdrawal distress, has been dispensed in clinics. This is a drastic departure from past government programs because it recognizes the drug addict as a patient and not necessarily a criminal. Furthermore, the panaceas about "cure" are replaced by the more realistic notion that this intense craving is difficult to overcome. Furthermore, the effects of methadone last from 24 to 36 hours in contrast to heroin whose effects endure for about 4 to 6 hours. Thus, experts recognized that the establishment of methadone maintenance clinics would eliminate the addict's recourse to theft or prostitution. These clinics are administered by medical doctors who prescribe the methadone to registered addicts. The methadone maintenance clinics have elicited a favorable response from many addicts, who recognized that this was one way of receiving the drugs free, and of hastening their resumption of a somewhat normal life, including retention of a job.

Synanon: Milieu and Group Therapy

Synanon is a form of milieu therapy in which group pressure becomes a lever to counteract the individual addict's craving for the drug.[29] It aims to reorient the addict to abstain, by the rewarding satisfaction of group approval, acceptance, and higher status. This self-help organization, which consists of former addicts, seeks to socialize a private individual's desire to abstain from the opiate into a shared form of behavior in a group whose core norm is abstinence from the drug. The series of steps taken in instilling abstinence begins with abstinence as a practice. The new member is deprived of all his personal possessions and has the lowest status as a recruit in this social system. His capacity to adapt by following orders successfully contributes to his advancement in this social system. The enforced group credo is that while a new participant might not agree with all that is said to him, he must react as if all the demands are true. By his abstinence, he is rewarded socially by group praise. The

29. Lewis Yablonsky, *The Tunnel Back Synanon* (New York: The Macmillan Company, 1965).

group provides the reason and rationalizations to justify his abstinence, and to denounce and forbid any favorable reactions to drug-taking. He is removed from his former associates who were addicts, may not talk to newcomers because it might divert them to talking about the drug, thus restimulating their desire to renew their habit.

In the conversations that ensue, called seminars, of which synanon is a corruption, the addict must talk against taking drugs, since his reorientation is crucial to his abstinence. Although synanon had made claims that up to 90 percent of its members have abstained, these claims may be overstated, because some addicts who were unable to tolerate the regimen dropped out.[30]

Education for Prevention

Education for prevention uses the mass media and the school to avert the very use of drugs. Celebrities such as athletes and actors make pleas in the way of commercials, warning of the dangers of drugs. These spot announcements supposedly would reorient youths who want to emulate successful athletes away from the use of drugs. There is no estimate of the effects of such announcements in deterring individuals from the use of drugs. The argument is that if these mass techniques can sell everything from soap to high political office, such short talks can also "sell" an aversion to the use of drugs.

The more direct preventive effort is to educate the children in the schools about the adverse effects of drugs. Despite the diligence of this effort, its effects thus far have been negative because children, in their subsequent behavior, become more curious about experimenting with drugs. Thus, at first inspection, it appears that

"educating" children about drugs fails to prevent their subsequent drug abuse. But this approach may also indicate that the methods of education are inadequate and therefore failed to reach their intended goals.

Suppression of the Drug Traffic

One of the basic problems of control of drugs is suppression of its illegal traffic. By preventing the drugs from reaching the addicts the law enforcement agents would thus deprive the traffickers from enormous sums of money. Traffic in drugs involves a long and secretive journey from the place of planting to the pusher. Generally, the opium is planted and harvested in Turkey, probably shipped to Marseilles where it is processed into morphine and perhaps into heroin, and from there, by diverse and devious routes, smuggled into the United States. The Narcotics Bureau has striven to apprehend the traffickers at points along the route. Despite increasing vigilance, the drugs were smuggled in. Finally, it was decided to pay the Turkish government for the opium crop. Despite this effective step, heroin from another point, East Asia, keeps coming into the country, with shipments continually being detected and confiscated.[31]

With these many pronged efforts to reduce the traffic and the use of opiates, some

30. See Rita Volkman and Donald B. Cressey, "Differential Association and the Rehabilitation of Drug Addicts," *American Journal of Sociology* (September, 1963), 49:2:129-143.

31. Permanent Subcommittee on Investigations of the Committee on Government Operations, U.S. Senate, *Organized Crime and Illicit Traffic*, Part 3, pp. 764, 765; Rufus King, "Narcotic Drug Laws and Enforcement Policies," *Law and Contemporary Problems* (Winter, 1957), 22:120-124.

impact and effect have been achieved; but the opiate distribution persists, and preventive and suppressive efforts continue to be urgent.

The Dilemma of Marihuana

Since research has shown that marihuana is not addictive nor necessarily more harmful than liquor or alcohol, the dilemma concerns whether to legalize it or so to reduce the penalty as to render it a misdemeanor? Marihuana is used by millions of people, many of them adults. One estimate of those who have used marihuana at least once reaches about 20 million. Marihuana is easily grown, hence readily accessible, and difficult to control. Furthermore, a contra-norm segment among many youths and even adults have so consistently flouted the law that they view it as informally acceptable, somewhat the same way that adults reacted during the period of the Volstead Act when the use of alcohol was prohibited. Since arrest affects only some users of marihuana, it is almost discriminatory as to who are arrested and sentenced.

It is necessary to determine what should be done about marihuana and youth. Legalizing marihuana would not be a wise alternative for youth. It would heighten its acceptability and increase its accessibility. Since it is at least as harmful as tobacco, it could have long-range harmful effects as well as creating short-range difficulties. Perhaps one realistic recourse is to consider its use a misdemeanor, for which the indi-

vidual should be restrained but not so heavily penalized as to affect his life course.

For Further Reading

Ausubel, David P. *Drug Addiction.* New York: Random House, Inc., 1966.
    This brief book analyzes the physiological, psychological and sociological aspects of drug addiction in a clear and thoughtful way.
Coles, Robert, Brenner, Joseph H., and Meagher. *Drugs and Youth.* New York: Liveright,
    This book, written by two doctors and a lawyer, tries to clarify the physiological, psychiatric and legal facts of the different types of drugs,, including heroin, marihuana, and LSD, as these affect young people.
Lindesmith, Alfred. *Addiction and Opiates.* Chicago: Aldine Publishing Company, 1968.
    This early analysis of drug addiction characterizes the onset of drug addication as resulting from relating the cessation of withdrawal symptoms to the opiate.
Maurer, David W., Vogel, Victor H. *Narcotics and Narcotic Addiction.* Springfield, Illinois: Charles C Thomas, Publishers, 1954.
    A discussion of the personality needs and the culture of the narcotics addict.
Schur, Edwin M. *Narcotic Addiction in Britain and America.* Bloomington, Indiana: Indiana University, 1963.
    A comparative analysis of the reactions to and treatment of drug addicts in the United States and Great Britain. The author inclines to support some of the constructive policies in Great Britain.
Solomon, David, ed. *The Marihuana Papers.* New York: New American Library, 1966.
    This selection of articles represents some of the competent studies on marihuana, dispels some of the myths connected with marihuana and clarifies the central facts of this drug.

4 | Sexual Deviance: Male Homosexuality

HOMOSEXUALITY as one type of sexual deviance has become increasingly tolerated by the heterosexual community. The open discussion of sexuality generally, as well as of homosexuality, has increased the degree of tolerance concerning this aspect of deviant behavior, so that homosexuals are less likely to be discriminated against in employment and in social life. The publicity by organized homosexual groups for equal rights has served to change some negative stereotypes about them as perverts. Also, studies of homosexuals have become more frequent and of greater depth, thus leading to further understanding.[1] Our discussion of homosexuality as a form of deviance includes (1) the definition and estimated extent of homosexuality, (2) its stereotypes, (3) its development and identification, (4) its subculture and (5) the role of homosexuals in contemporary society.

HOMOSEXUALITY DEFINED

Individuals who participate in homosexual activity or its intermittent practice without climax are not necessarily homosexuals. Boys, during the latency period, engage in homosexual play but are not homosexuals, and do not necessarily become homosexuals.

The homosexual is one who has a sexual preference for persons of the same sex and who privately or overtly considers himself a homosexual. This sexual desire for persons of the same gender as sex objects may be exclusive or it may be partial. Thus, some persons are exclusively homosexual, while others are bi-sexual, finding both males and females acceptable sex objects.

Situational homosexuals such as persons in prisons may resort to homosexual practices during their deprivation of the opposite sex but revert to heterosexuality when the opportunity exists.

THE EXTENT OF HOMOSEXUALITY

The frequency of homosexuality can at best be estimated. One estimate reaches back to Kinsey's survey of male sexuality in 1948. He reported that 37 percent of his male subjects had experienced homosexual action leading to climax, while another 13 percent had homosexual experience without climax. On the basis of a seven point scale from heterosexuality as one, to exclusive homosexuality as six or seven, ten percent were homosexual for at least three years, 25 percent were more than incidentally homosexual, but 4 percent or 26,631 males were exclusive homosexuals.[1] A recent (1973) survey of sex behavior among American males by Guildhall associates, sponsored by Playboy Enterprises, also revealed that even less than 4 percent of the American males were exclusively homosexuals, although a large number participated in homosexual play, particularly during childhood, and this occurred despite a more permissive attitude toward premarital sex. The methods of this survey, however, appear questionable.

In single sex institutions such as prisons the percentage of homosexuals is considerably higher. For example, Clemmer reported that of 2,300 male prisoners, 30 percent were bi-sexual and 10 percent were exclusively homosexual.[2]

In attempting to estimate the extent of homosexuality, it is necessary to consider that many pairs of males who live together would be reluctant to disclose their homosexuality. On the other hand, homosexual activists exaggerate their numbers. At best, because of its privacy, atypicality, and varying definitions from bi-sexuality to exclusive homosexuality, the extent of homosexuality can at best be an approximate estimate.

STEREOTYPES OF HOMOSEXUALS

The homosexual, by the very nature of his sexual deviance, creates sustained negative stereotypes in the minds of the general community. He is considered a pervert whose behavior is immoral by reason of its deviate and promiscuous character, and even sinful. Some regard his behavior as consistent with a process of emotional and moral degeneracy which reflects the very "decay of the society itself," because of a sensate lust for new pleasures, and the loss of masculine identity. But homosexuals regard the prevailing moral codes and stereotypes as a compendium of prejudices on the part of heterosexuals. Homosexuals contend that their morals are similar to those of heterosexuals except for their sex practices.[3]

From the vantage point of another stereotype, homosexuals are considered as afflicted products of mental illness. Their very homosexual behavior is considered "sick." The American Psychiatric Association in its *Diagnostic and Statistical Manual of 1968*, diagnosed homosexuality as a mental illness.[4] Homosexuals, contend, however, that such medical and psychiatric references are degrading and inaccurate. They deny that they are "sick heterosexuals" with an overlay of homosexuality, but rather, they assert that they are as healthy physically and mentally as heterosexuals. They disavow the psychiatric evaluation of therapy as a "solution" to their condition. Some investigators contend that psychiatrists and other clinicians regard homosexuals as sick because they see only "sick ones" in their practice. Healthy homosexuals do not visit

1. See Harry M. Dank, "The Homosexuals," *Outsiders, USA*, eds. Dan Spiegel and Patricia Keith Spiegel (San Francisco: Rinehart Press, 1973) pp. 270-297; John Gagnon and William Simon, "Homosexuality: The Formulation of a Sociological Perspective," *Approaches to Deviance*, Mark Lefton et al., eds. (New York: Appleton-Century-Crofts, 1968) pp. 349-361.
2. Alfred C. Kinsey et al., *Sexual Behavior in the Human Male* (Philadelphia: W. B. Saunders Co., 1948). See also, Evelyn Hooker, "The Homosexual Community," *Sexual Deviance*, ed. John Gagnon and William Simon (New York: Harper & Row, Publisher, 1967) pp. 167-184.
3. See Robert R. Bell, *Social Deviance* (Homewood, Illinois: The Dorsey Press, 1971) pp. 248-284.
4. American Psychiatric Association, *Diagnostic and Statistical Manual of Mental Disorders* (Washington, D. C., 1968) 2nd edition. See also: 3rd edition.

therapists. As a consequence of their vigorous and apparently sound protests, the American Psychiatric Association in 1973 revised their diagnostic definition of homosexuality to that of a mental illness of a divergent orientation of a sexual character. In effect, they denied that homosexuality is an "illness."

Consistently, the National Association of Mental Health reported that homosexuality *per se* does not constitute a specific "mental or emotional disease," or threaten the health of the individual or society. In brief, despite a pervasive stereotype depicting homosexuality as an illness, homosexuals consider themselves to be as mentally and emotionally sound and as clinically normal as heterosexuals and have influenced the psychiatric and other clinical professions to agree with them.

This was demonstrated dramatically by Dr. Howard Brown, first health services commissioner in Mayor Lindsay's Cabinet in New York City. In an address before 600 physicians at a symposium, he admitted candidly that he had been a homosexual for many years. He did not mention his homosexual identity prior to his appointment as health commissioner because he felt his appointment would have been denied. He kept his homosexuality a secret during his 18 months in office because he knew he might have been discharged or forced to resign. He eventually resigned because of his fear that a columnist, Drew Pearson, was about to write an exposé of the homosexuals in Mayor Lindsay's cabinet and administration.[5]

The third stereotype pertains to the effeminacy of male homosexuals whose walk, talk, and general mannerisms supposedly resemble those of a woman. As a consequence, they are stereotyped as "fairies," "fruits," "fags," or "queers," identifiable by their manner. But many homosexuals have contrasting values; femininity is scorned and masculinity prized. Some homosexuals, in fact, exaggerate their masculinity to attract other homosexuals, and deride the "Nellies," whom they depreciate. It has been emphasized that virile cowboys and Indians in the 19th century were frequently homosexuals, in part because of the absence of women, and also because the homosexual tendency was confirmed. In brief, in the "gay subculture," masculinity is a valued commodity which men cultivate; and many consider masculinity superior to femininity. In the homosexual hierarchy, the masculine prototype is the aggressor—active and superior—while the feminine prototype is passive and subordinate.

Although these stereotypes characterize homosexuals in a somewhat negative and distorted way, the fact is that many persons are far removed from and ignorant of homosexuality. But stereotypes also serve as guidelines for their own sex-appropriate behavior. In other words, heterosexuals feel that if they were to resort to homosexuality it would represent mental illness or a perverted act, or indicate effeminacy.

Kitsuse in this context has analyzed the reactions of persons to what they construed to be contacts with homosexuals. Kitsuse inferred from the reactions by heterosexuals to homosexuals that their conceptions of sex-appropriate and sex-inappropriate behavior led them to interpret a variety of behavioral forms as indicative of forms of

5. *Chicago Sun-Times* (October 4, 1973) p. 96. See also: D. S. Barley, *Homosexuality and the Western Christian Tradition* (London: Longmans-Green, 1955); M. Hoffman, *The Gay World: Male Homosexuality and the Social Evil* (New York: Basic Books, Inc., Publishers, 1968).

sexual deviation. He also found that an individual's sexual "normality" may be made problematic by interpretations of others, and that the significant fact is not the actions of individuals defined as deviant, "but rather the interpretations others make of their behaviors, whatever those behaviors may be."[6]

The fact is that the homosexual overture threatens the heterosexual. Whatever the variety of gestures by homosexuals or by others construed as homosexual, when the act suggests homosexuality, it arouses defensive reactions by males to protect their sexual self-esteem. The reactions of heterosexuals respond to basic clues (acts) which violate the norms of appropriate heterosexual behavior. If a homosexual reaches for a male's privates, clearly the reality of the deviance is not in the interpretation but in the very act itself as a variation from a general norm. Should this behavior be permitted, and not considered deviant, the regulatory sex norms which the individual has internalized and by which he abides would break down. Thus, the stereotypes in the minds of the general heterosexual population represent not only their social distance and hence ignorance of homosexuals, but are also defensive guidelines for sustaining their heterosexual identity, beyond which they forbid themselves to trespass.

THE DEVELOPMENT OF THE HOMOSEXUAL

The developmental studies of homosexuality usually conform to the clinical stereotype that his sexual deviance results from personality instability. Thus the aim of these studies is to ascertain the differences in family organization and parent-child relations of homosexuals and heterosexuals. These developmental differences, however,

do not explain the genesis of homosexuality. Bene compared 83 self-confessed homosexual men and 84 married men in terms of their early parent-child relations. Consistent with the findings of studies by Schofield and others, she found that the homosexuals more frequently than the heterosexuals had bad relations with fathers who were ineffectual parents and who did not serve as role-models for them. On the other hand and inconsistent with other studies, they were found to be less frequently attached to their mothers than heterosexuals, less frequently over-indulged by them, and less frequently apt to consider them role-models. Briefly, from the findings of this intensive inquiry, it appears that homosexuals did not differ significantly from heterosexuals in their early parent-child relations.[7]

SEXUAL ESTRANGEMENT FROM THE OPPOSITE SEX

Since the homosexual usually develops amidst his heterosexual parents and siblings, he must be involved in basic social processes in addition to biological conditions which contribute to his becoming motivated sexually toward persons of the same sex. These social processes become fixated during childhood, youth, or early adulthood, when the individual realizes that he is a homosexual. The incubation of this psychosexual development occurs while the parents, es-

6. John Kitsuse, "Societal Reaction to Deviant Behavior," *Social Problems*, 9:3 (Winter, 1962) pp. 247-256; Michael Schofield, *Sociological Aspects of Homosexuality* (Boston: Little Brown and Company, 1965).
7. See *Ibid.* Eva Bene, "On the Genesis of Male Homosexuality," *British Journal of Psychiatry* (September, 1965), pp. 803-811.

pecially the mother, although the father also, is perhaps a significant figure.

In its inception, one phase of homosexual development antecedes the homosexual's birth. The parents, prior to the child's birth, may want a girl rather than a boy. Consistently, during early childhood the mother trains and identifies the child as a girl, emphasizing effeminate qualities and the female role. The result is that the boy becomes a "sissy" and eventually may be coerced into homosexual relations by his peers, conduct to which he may respond sexually with mild or minimal protest. These boyhood experiences may then confirm and fixate his homophilic tendencies.

In this psychosexual process, the individual becomes psychosexually estranged from a masculine role and a masculine identity; but the learning of homosexuality comes from his sexual experiences with his male peers.

Another process ensues when the mother becomes "seductive and alluring" to the son, who may react by feelings of incestuous guilt over his sexual desires for the mother and consequently develop an intense inhibition toward the mother as a sex object; this may expand into a sexual inhibition regarding women generally. Thus he may become susceptible to respond to men as sex objects. This process may influence the individual's sex attitudes without his being aware of his psychosexual tendencies. During adolescence he may then realize his predispositions, which may become reinforced by homosexual contact and ensuing gratification with one or more schoolmates, thus becoming fixated and sustained.

Another line of development among homosexuals may come as a learning process among peers who are isolated from the opposite sex and turn to homosexuality.

Young participants may become so involved emotionally that they may regard themselves as homosexuals even though some may be bi-sexual.

A fourth line of development arises from the frustrations encountered in their sex relations with women. Some men are made to feel inadequate in the sexual process, others are rejected, ridiculed, or deserted. Eventually these individuals despair of having satisfactory relations with women and turn to men as alternatives.

THE SOCIAL IDENTITY OF THE HOMOSEXUAL: "COMING OUT"

The person who accedes to his sexual inclinations toward males may identify himself as an overt or public homosexual, in a distinct social process known as "coming out."[8] He finds that his identity as a homosexual can be made known to other homosexuals in places where he is visible, such as a "gay bar." His identity as a homosexual, moreover, becomes acceptable to him, so that he sheds the stereotypes that he is "queer" or a "pervert." He feels the need to demonstrate to himself that he can behave as a homosexual. Thus he may venture into a "gay bar" for the first time to meet other homosexuals and to feel that he is among his own kind. He may realize that his initial experiences with like males are sometimes referred to as the "honeymoon," because his sexual activities may become very frequent and intense. The "coming out" process also means that the homosexual will no longer consider marriage and the responsibilities of parenthood, as would a heterosexual. And it means

8. Harry M. Dank, "Coming Out in the Gay World," *Psychiatry* (1971) 34:180-197.

that he will focus his activities upon his homosexual practices and associations.[8]

In a survey of 386 self-identified homosexuals, Dank reported that about age 21 was the average for homosexual identity, although 12 percent were between ages eight and twelve, 35 percent between ages fifteen and nineteen, and about 31 percent between twenty and twenty-four, and 22 percent age twenty-five and older.

Homosexuals called "closet queens" do not wish to define themselves as homosexuals. Some may marry, but after an interim of agonizing they may renounce their marriage by divorce, and "come out" as avowed homosexuals.

THE SOCIAL ROLE OF THE HOMOSEXUAL

Homosexuals necessarily are conspicuous in a heterosexual society and have a distinct social role.[9] Their homosexual role takes precedence over their other social roles. Homosexuals voluntarily restrict their associations to other homosexuals, among whom they can be completely accepted.

But homosexuals in high status positions ranging from ministers to military officers may conceal their sexual inclinations by "passing." They resort to clandestine ways to appease their sexual impulses, such as visiting gay bars in distant cities on business trips, seeking homosexual contacts in washrooms, or visiting male prostitutes. Persons who "pass" frequently are married and conceal their psychosexual identity in order to retain their jobs.[10] For example, a dean of a college was arrested for consenting to homosexual practices while in a hotel in another city, and lost his job. Jenkins, an advisor to President Johnson, was arrested for homosexuality in a YMCA men's washroom, an experience which ended his

federal appointment. The higher the homosexual's position the greater is his tendency to conceal his homosexuality.

The reasons reported for maintaining their secrecy as homosexuals were a wish to avoid social ridicule (22 cases), fear of loss of job or when self-employed, (22 cases) inability to recruit clients, (20 cases), desire to protect family and friends (18 cases). The cases add to more than 40 because some subjects gave more than one reason for their reluctance to assume the social role of the homosexual. Since 1956, when this study was published, it is evident that homosexuals have become more open in identifying themselves, because of the vigorous publicity which homophile associations have made, with the heterosexual community placed on the defensive for its manifest intolerance.[11]

TYPES OF HOMOSEXUAL ROLES

Humphrey has classified homosexual roles into (1) trade, (2) ambisexuals, (3) gay guys and (4) closet queens.[12] Evidently, he formulated this typology from the habitués of the public washrooms or "tearooms," where they can encounter other anonymous persons for instant sex in a single and rapid experience which usually involves fellatio. There are other settings for this type of activity including, balconies of movie theatres, automobiles, behind bushes; but public washrooms provide the setting that per-

9. Dank, "The Homosexuals."
10. J. Star, "The Homosexual Couple," *Look* (January 26, 1971) pp. 69-81.
11. Maurice Leznoff and William A. Westley, "The Homosexual Community," *Social Problems* (April, 1956) 3:257-63.
12. Laud Humphreys, *Tearoom Trade* (Chicago: Aldine Publishing Company, 1970) pp. 104, 105, 108-130.

mits encounters with the least involvement. Nevertheless, the majority of arrests for homosexuality are made in the public washroom.

Trade Role

The "trade" role of homosexual consists predominantly of men who are married or have been married. Most of them were truck drivers, machine operators, or clerical workers. These men have a shakey marriage and have virtually ceased having sex relations with their wives. They seek a quick, impersonal, and inexpensive outlet. At one time, these individuals might have gratified themselves in a brothel, but such conditions are no longer available, so they turn to men.

They avoid any involvement in the homosexual subculture, speak minimally while in the washroom, and desire only quick gratification in an anonymous sex encounter. The trade types are lonely, isolated figures, knowing few if any other homosexuals and having few, if any, friends.

Ambisexuals

Ambisexuals have homosexual friendships, with whom they become involved in a learning experience. They learn which public rest rooms are popular, where the police are alerted, and what officers are seeking payoffs. Furthermore, their tearoom encounters are reinforced by their friendship network.

Since they are in the middle class and upper middle class, they have more to lose by their exposure, but they also have more means to protect themselves. Thus, the bisexuals do conceive of themselves as homosexuals in part, although they are capable of heterosexual relations. And they are also involved in social relations with other homosexuals, so that they participate in the homosexual subculture.

"Gay Guys"

The "Gay Guys" are in the forefront of the homosexual subculture. Largely young and single they are confirmed homosexuals, are knowledgeable about the ways of the gay world, about places to meet, strategies in the tearooms, cautions to avoid the entrapment of police decoys. Many are educated and intelligent. Half of the "gay guys" studied by Humphreys were college graduates, and all but one were at least part-time students. As students, their median income was low. These "gay types" are socially successful and claim to have many friends, regard their sexual drives as normal, and tend to be satisfied with this aspect of their lives. They speak of "marrying" a man they love and settling down. When two men are so attracted, as a demonstration of a lasting bond between them, they exchange "pinky rings." They fit closely the stereotype of the effeminate homosexual. Some try to avoid the public washroom, because they want a more durable type of sexual relation with one male if possible; but their relations actually are largely transient.

"Closet Queens"

Closet queens as we have pointed out keep their identification hidden, have few friends among homosexuals, and are covert in their sexual activities. Some prefer teenage boys and act as lone wolves. They prefer the costs and danger of soliciting the corner youths to actively associating with the known homosexuals in gay bars and other hangouts.

The Homosexual Community and Its Subculture

The "gay" community is not territorially based. It is concentrated in its hangouts and network of social relationships. It has its selected meeting places in bars, public baths, coffee shops, restaurants, and public washrooms. Homosexuals also favor certain stores and barber shops. They have newspapers, and homophile associations, a special argot and a network of informal associations, cliques, and groups. As the homosexual becomes incorporated into this subsociety, his interests become focussed upon his informal associations and groups, among whom gossip and friendships ensue.[13]

"Gay" bars are crucial meeting places for homosexuals. Located predominantly in large cities, they are concentrated in specific areas, so that clients can drift through several bars in the course of a night. In San Francisco and in Los Angeles, over fifty gay bars were noted. Hooker estimated that in a large, successful bar in Los Angeles on a Saturday night between 10:00 P.M. and 2:00 A.M. about 1,000 men drifted through.[14] At these bars the homosexuals make contacts with others for arranging sexual liaisons called "one-night stands." A pair who eye each other may be seeking a knowing glance and smile or other suitable gestures which mean an agreement for homosexual activity. But at these bars, friends and acquaintances also gather to gossip, to find out about invitations to parties, or of impending important happenings, as well as warnings of police activities. The cliques and groups who meet may vary by socioeconomic strata, occupation, and taste.[15]

The bath house is another site for having sex relations by fellatio, with very little to distract them. Thus, homosexuals may frequent a bath house for this explicit purpose.

The homosexual subculture also functions as a buffer against a hostile heterosexual community. The common orientation of the participants in the latter category is manifested by their similar interests and their discussions of common problems. They seek to diminish guilt that homosexuals might acquire. Accepted among their own kind, they collectively reinforce each other's rationalizations of the satisfactory nature of their differences.

Deviants of this type who associate with one another have a certain loyalty. They drift into occupations where they will not be discriminated, with the result that certain fields may have relatively high percentages of homosexuals.

They may form cohesive social groups who constitute their focal social relationships. The "queen" or leader of the group provides a place where homosexuals meet, helps those in distress, functions as a liaison in making sexual contacts, controls the admission of new members, and admonishes members concerning predatory persons, "the dirt," who can harm them.[16] Homosexuals differentiate between sex relations and friendships. Some do not like to mingle the two.[17]

13. Dank, "Homosexuals"; Leznoff and Westley, "The Homosexual Community"; Hooker, "The Homosexual Community"; Bell, *Social Deviance*.

14. Hooker, "The Homosexual Community."

15. Leznoff and Westley, "The Homosexual Community"; Dank, "Homosexuals."

16. Leznoff and Westley, "The Homosexual Community."

17. Laud Humphreys, *Tearoom Trade* (Chicago: Aldine-Atherton Inc., 1970).

The "one-night stand" is the usual mode of transient sex relations; it is experienced without obligation or commitment. The active homosexual experiences dozens of such acts within a few days or a week. Generally, the youthful, masculine appearing male tends to be attractive, although for some the feminine appearance is also attractive. As the individual ages, his attraction declines, so that liaisons are more difficult to arrange. At a certain stage, he may pay his partner in a virtual prostitute-like relationship. The homosexual clearly distinguishes the sexual liaison from a friendship, although some homosexuals, because of mutual attraction and convenience, arrange to live together as "married couples."

The "gay community" on a level of social relations consists of cliques and groups who are linked together by common interests, orientations, obstacles, that is by common problems. Within this social world, they may also develop bitter jealousies and rivalries. But in general, homosexuals feel that they can "let their hair down" among their own kind and discuss their problems openly and in their distinctive argot.[18]

Homosexuals also have formal homophile associations which are designed to publicize their image in favorable light, to depict themselves as normal persons "with a difference," who are persecuted or at least discriminated against like any other minority group. Their aim is to break down prejudices existng in the general heterosexual community, and to attain the tolerance for homosexuals which other minority groups have achieved.

THE CHANGING ROLE OF THE HOMOSEXUAL IN CONTEMPORARY SOCIETY

The role of the homosexual is in a state of transition from the status of being re-

garded as an immoral pervert and law violator, to one who can and should be tolerated if not accepted by the larger heterosexual communty. Although the homosexual can be arrested in 45 states for violating the law, in many northern and western states, these laws are less rigorously enforced than they were in the past. Liberalization of the laws concerning homosexuality is consistent with the low visibility of homosexual behavior, the relative indifference of the pubilc toward homosexuality, as well as difficulties in enforcing existing laws. The most significant aspect of these laws is that it increases the homosexual's vulnerability to blackmail. The homosexual view is that sex relations between consenting adults is a private matter and should not be subject to legal accountability. In several states this view has become increasingly acceptable.

Another consideration pertains to homosexuality as a basis for prejudice and discrimination in employment and other areas. The goal of homosexuals is to be accepted despite their homosexuality, which would be stated openly rather than being concealed and an object of potential blackmail.

On the other hand, the fact that a homosexual may try to make advances and impose upon young boys is considered a threat. This type of behavior, however, may be penalized, not necessarily because of its homosexual intent, but because it invades the rights of others by molestation or by forceful imposition.

In general, the more informed public opinion is about homosexuality and the more openly it is discussed, the more readily will tolerance for this form of behavior be

18. Dank, "The Homosexuals"; Bell, *Social Deviance*.

attained. As long as homosexuals can remain productive, law-abiding participants
in society and practice their homosexuality
with consenting adults, tolerance for their
behavior might exist.

For Further Reading

Churchill, Wainwright. *Homosexual Behavior
Among Males: A Cross-Cultural and Cross
Species Investigation.* New York: Hawthorn,
1967.
    Clear characterization of the practice of
homosexuality in diverse societies and its
extent of continuity with other animals.
Dank, Harry M. "Coming Out in the Gay
World," *Psychiatry,* 1971, 34, pp. 180-197.
    Describes clearly the process of attaining
identity as a homosexual.
Gagnon, John and Simon, William. "Homosexuality: The Formulation of a Sociological Perspective," *Approaches to Deviance,* pp. 349-
361. M. Lefton, et al., eds. New York: Appleton-Century-Crofts, 1968.
Hooker, Evelyn. "The Homosexual Community," *Sexual Deviance,* ed. John Gagnon and
William Simon. New York: Harper and Row,
Publishers, 1967, pp. 167-196.
    A knowledgable analysis of the institu-
tions and practices with the homosexual subculture.
Humphrey, Laud. *Tearoom Trade.* Chicago:
Aldine-Atherton, Inc., 1970.
    Analyzes the meeting and meeting places
of homosexuals, such as public rest rooms in
the total set of understandings and cultural
orientations among homosexuals.
Schur, Edwin. *Crimes Without Victims.* Englewood Cliffs, N. J.: Prentice-Hall, Inc., 1965.
    A discussion of the social and legal facets
of homosexuality in the light of their present
role in society.

5 | Mental Disorders and Deviance

MENTAL disorders pertain to widely diverse forms of behavior. Many disturbed people who can comport themselves within the norms of their social roles are considered socially normal. In fact, some disturbed persons fear social disapproval so intensely that they become overconformistic. Others may so inhibit their conflicts that their covert tensions result in psychosomatic disorders. Persons in a third category may be considered "off-beat," but within acceptable social limits, and hence are not viewed as deviant. Severely disordered persons who are deviant cannot control their impulsive behavior, which exceeds the limits of tolerance. They speak incoherently or irrationally, they are completely immobile or excessively agitated, they suffer memory lapses and identity distortions, have private views of social reality, hallucinate, whether in hearing voices or seeing visions.[1] But these forms of disordered behavior which people classify or frequently prejudge as "insane," reflect traditional stereotypes of the "insane."

This chapter deals with mental disorders as social phenomena and discusses: (1) their extent, (2) their diagnostic types and stereotypes, (3) socialization and estrangement processes contributing to mental disorders,

(4) social factors in psychoses, and (5) the control and rehabilitation of the mentally disordered.

THE EXTENT OF MENTAL DISORDERS

Estimates of the extent of mental disorders vary considerably. One estimate is that between nine and ten million people have disturbed personalities. Approximately one million persons are so severely disturbed as to become hospitalized or require psychiatric care, although the number of resident hospital patients at any given time is about one-half million.[2]

DIAGNOSTIC TYPES OF MENTAL DISORDERS

The two major categories of mental disorders are (1) neuroses and (2) psychoses. Neuroses, the more frequent of the two disorders, do not necessarily result in bizarre behavior, and such persons are not necessarily considered deviants. The basic neur-

1. S. Kirson Weinberg, ed., *Psychiatric Sociology: The Sociology of Mental Disorders* (Chicago: Aldine-Atherton Inc., 1967).
2. National Institute of Mental Health, *Patients in Mental Institutions, 1965.* (Washington D. C.: United States Government Printing Office, 1961), Publication No. 1091.

osis is anxiety, which arises from a person's confrontation with one or a series of threatening or dangerous conditions to which he cannot respond protectively or effectively, and which results in a feeling of helpless panic. To avert this disorganized anxiety his psychological flight of memory becomes a process of repression. His defensive reactions to the anxiety are (1) hysteria, or (2) obsessive compulsion. By physical and psychological means, the hysteric is able to deal with a threatening situation by escaping responsiblity for it. The obsessive, by repeated, circular worries, tries to re-do the experience; the compulsive repeats actions, such as the man fearing a burglar, who may repeatedly turn the knob of his door to reassure himself that it is locked. These disorders, while impairing the person's behavior in society, do not require hospitalization and hence usually are not labelled as deviant, unless perhaps informally.[3]

Psychoses differ from the neuroses by involving disorientation from social reality; they represent a more severe and pernicious form of personality disorganization.

The psychoses are divided into (1) personality or functional psychoses, including schizophrenia, manic-depressive, and paranoid disorders, and (2) organic psychoses which stem from some organic aberration or injury or organic change such as arteriosclerosis, paresis and alcoholic psychosis.

Personality or functional psychoses are severe forms of disorganization of the person. These psychoses usually reveal signs of disorientation, such as repudiation of social reality, especially by hallucinations and delusions, or private versions of "reality." Schizophrenia, the most frequent of the psychoses, is characterized by (1) disorientation, (2) withdrawal emotionally and

socially, and (3) disrupted thought-processes.

The manic-depressive psychoses include (1) mania, (2) depression and (3) cycles of mania and depression. Depressives are self-accusatory and self-depreciating persons who are immobilized or agitated by depressed feelings. The manic condition reveals scattered reactions and falsely elated notions. Our concern will be with personality or functional disorders, as we first characterize the stereotyped notions about mental disorders, then trace the processes of individual estrangement involved in the reactions of schizophrenics.

STEREOTYPES OF MENTAL DISORDER

Disordered behavior refers to a mentally and emotionally impaired or incapacitated condition. But we realize that this condition is relative, that shades of difference exist in the spectrum of disordered behavior ranging from the normal through the mild and severe neurotic to the extreme condition of the severe psychotic. In the nineteenth and the first half of the 20th centuries, the discontinuous dichotomy was between the insane—a legal term—and the sane. The insane or abnormal were in the asylum. The sane or normal were outside. The popular imagery of the insane asylum connoted stigma and dread. It was a "booby-hatch," and "nut-house." Inmates were regarded as dangerous persons who had to be confined because they were irresponsible, and who had to be watched and treated like children. In the mental hospital they were deprived of civil liberties, the right to vote, and to manage their prop-

3. S. Kirson Weinberg, *Society and Personality Disorders* (Englewood Cliffs, N. J.: Prentice-Hall Inc., 1952).

Table 5.1

**Type of Disordered Behavior By Evaluation
of Conformity and Deviance**

Type of Disorder	Predominant Conformity-Deviance Evaluation
1. Mild Neuroses	1. Conformity to Minor Deviance
2. Psychosomatic Disorders	2. Conformity to Minor Deviance
3. Neuroses	3. Conformity to Minor Deviance
4. Severe Neuroses, Some Paranoid Disorders	4. Minor Deviance, e.g., "Queer," "Strange," "Flaky." 2. Requires Treatment, 3. Afflicted Persons Participate in Society
5. Psychoses and Severe Neuroses	5. Marked Deviance Requires Hospitalization and Removal from Society

erty; they were forbidden to send or receive letters without inspection. Their very complaints were considered symptomatic of their insane conditions, rather than valid observations and grievances.

Psychotics, as insane, were viewed as a throwback in the evolutionary process, or a regression to a kind of childhood. Schizophrenics particularly were considered "born that way," and "once insane, always insane," as being beyond complete recovery. They were viewed as potentially hostile, aggressive, and hence dangerous persons. Nourished by continual reports in newspapers and books, people believed that whenever hideous crimes or assaults were committed, this was the work of an insane person. Thus, insanity was viewed as the source of personal crimes, an attitude diffused in the mass notion that all insane were somehow potentially given to committing assaults. It was not acknowledged until later that most mentally ill persons were gentler than normal people, and that more assaults and homicides were committed by clinically normal and sane persons than by psychotics. But the fear necessarily persisted that psychotics, as insane, were not attuned to society, nor contained by its modes of social control. It was believed that they were motivated by their own notions, were unpredictable and hence untrustworthy,[4] because they were not responsible. Instead, many were child-like and desocialized. Psychotics, by their desocialized behavior, present a lack or loss of what we associate with being human: the ability to communicate, the capability of self-control of one's impulses, and of self-orientation. This fear of desocialization, of being inhuman, of losing self-control, seemed to be the bases of the stereotype attitude which required some psychotics to be removed from society.[5]

After World War II, lessons learned from the emotionally disturbed soldiers combined with the growth of psychiatry, led to a redefinition of "insane," replacing it by the expression "mentally ill." Some stereotypes that the onset of psychosis was not limited also began to change. First, it was found

4. See Erving Goffman, "The Moral Career of the Mental Patient," *Psychiatry: Journal for the Study of Interpersonal Processes* (May, 1959), 22, pp. 123-131.
5. Erving Goffman, *Asylums* (Chicago: Aldine-Atherton Publishing Company, 1962); H. Warren Dunham and S. Kirson Weinberg. *Culture of the State Mental Hospital* (Detroit: Wayne State University Press, 1960).

to any category of people. Seemingly stable persons also could break down, as was evident among the soldiers in the war. Second, psychoses were not only a result of genetic predisposition but also of intensified biological and social stresses. Third, disordered behavior had varied degrees of intensity, from the neuroses through the psychoses. Fourth, psychotics could readily recover socially, as was evident among the transient psychotics in combat, who manifested psychotic tendencies for a brief period, then improved. Fifth, some psychotics were not necessarily dangerous and could be trusted on the outside. Sixth, they could be considered "sick" like other physically sick people, and with improvement could participate in society without being stigmatized, in contrast to the "always insane" traditional stereotype.[6] Seventh, the stigma of mental illness declined and softer terms were used more extensively.

The change in these notions and social stereotypes contributed to the changed treatment of and reactions toward the mentally disordered. It meant that such persons could be treated in the clinic in the home community, rather than forcibly confined to a mental hospital. It meant greater acceptance of the former mental patient. It developed, as we shall see, into the "community psychiatry" approach. The role of social processes in contributing to psychoses also was more clearly understood and accepted, as we see in the discord and estrangement experienced by the schizophrenics who tend to be both psychotic and deviant.

DEVELOPMENT OF SCHIZOPHRENIC BEHAVIOR: THE PROCESS OF ESTRANGEMENT

Schizophrenics frequently experience conflict and rejection in one or several groups such as family, peers, members of the opposite sex, and work associates. These conflicts may contribute to the eventual onset of the disorder.

The Family

In general, parent-child relations, especially mother-children relations, involve conflicts at an early age, which result in a lowered self-evaluation by the child. Mothers of schizophrenics may be directly or subtly dominating and rejecting. Some intimidate their children, suppress their initiative, impose distorted goals upon them. Many schizophrenics, during childhood, strived to fulfill demands that would please the mother or parents, rather than satisfy their own needs. Sometimes, parents set unattainable goals for their children, who as a result, experience the sting of failure. The mothers who were the crucial parent-figures were usually emotionally unstable, and influenced their children accordingly. Tietze, who studied 25 mothers of schizophrenics, reported that all were hostile and domineering, but their manner differed from open and direct to subtle and indirect. The mothers who resorted to indirect forms of domination were more destructive to the children, and confused them. Hence they encountered more difficulty with rebelling children. Ensnared by these techniques, the fathers became obligated to follow her demands. In one instance, a mother dominated her three daughters, not by shouting but by crying, convenient headaches, and fainting spells.

6. Thomas J. Scheff, "The Societal Reaction to Deviance: Ascriptive Elements in the Psychiatric Screening of Mental Patients in Midwestern State," *Social Problems* (Spring, 1964) 11:4:401-413.

Two of the three daughters became schizophrenic, and one was afflicted with an ulcerative colitis, which may arise from personality conflicts as a psychosomatic disorder.[7] Despert reported that in 19 out of 29 cases the mothers were aggressive, oversolicitous, and over-anxious about their children, and that they aroused anxiety into the children.[8] Lidz found that 45 of 50 parents were unstable, experienced marital strain, were domineering and possessive of their children, and restricted their social latitude to develop.[9] As a consequence, the children, when they did rebel, withdrew emotionally. The fathers in these cases were usually docile, according to Despert, but austere and also strict in their demands.

In some instances, however, the mothers treated the preschizophrenic child differently than her other children. A mother may have focussed her discontent upon the child who eventually was afflicted, but not on the others. The child thus affected may be unwanted and rejected, whereas the others may be wanted and accepted. Lu, in comparing the maternal relations with a schizophrenic son and his nonschizophrenic sibling, noted that the mother's relations were almost the opposite for the two sons, as can be seen in Table 5.2. The nonschizophrenic was wanted, the schizophrenic, as a baby, was unwanted.[10]

But the mother also influences the peer relations of the child and youth and thus restrains him so that this affects his capacity to fit into the peer group. Relations with peers are affected because of residual effects upon their personalities as consequences of the harmful relations with the parents. Wynne and his co-researchers found that from childhood, (1) the parents' domination of the child's attention interfered with his capacity for goal-oriented

7. Trude Tietze, "A Study of Mothers of Schizophrenic Patients," *Psychiatry* (February, 1949), 12:1, pp. 55-65.
8. Louise Despert, "Schizophrenia in Children," *Psychiatric Quarterly* (July, 1938), 12:3, pp. 366-371.
9. Ruth W. Lidz and Theodore Lidz, "The Family Environment of Schizophrenic Patients," *American Journal of Psychiatry* (November, 1949), 106:5, pp. 343-345.
10. Yi Chuang Lu, "Contradictory Parental Expectations in Schizophrenia," *Archives of General Psychiatry* (March, 1962), 6:2, pp. 219-234.

Table 5.2

Comparison of Maternal Attitudes Between Her Schizophrenic and Normal Sons

Schizophrenic: David	Normal: Paul
1. Not a Planned Baby	1. Planned
2. Not a Wanted Child [Born during worst financial conditions of Family]	2. Wanted Child
3. Mother was Tense and Worried at time of Birth	3. Mother was Normal and Relaxed
4. Marital and Sex Relations were strained	4. Marital and Sex Relations were normal
5. A Big Baby: Hard Delivery	5. A Small Baby: Easy Delivery
6. Both parents wanted a Girl; Disappointed by a Boy	6. Didn't Care Whether Boy or Girl
7. Spent Considerable Time with Him	7. Spent less Time with Him
8. Made Very Dependent on Mother	8. Not Dependent on Mother

and purposive behavior, (2) the parent-child relationships were erratic and confusing, (3) the child, reacting to these inconsistent relations, experienced an underlying feeling of meaninglessness and emptiness, (4) the family, by a process of collusion, denied the anxiety-creating experiences. These hostile and deceptive forms of relations in which the appearance of harmony covers and obscures the underlying destructive and manipulating tendencies which the mother expressed to the child.[11] Thus the child lacks the capacity for healthy, normal, sound interpersonal relations, is easily manipulated and intimidated by others.

The potential schizophrenic, as a consequence of parental relations, became too confused and intimidated to defy his mother and father. Instead, his estrangement assumed a protective social posture, with emotional withdrawal from parental demands.

Peer Relations

Although some psychotics form and maintain peer relations during childhood and youth, many schizophrenics seem to operate on the fringe of the peer group, or they are estranged and isolated from their peers. Clausen and Kohn, in a study of 45 schizophrenics, reported 34 or 75.5 percent were either isolated or played with friends occasionally, as contrasted with only 4 percent of the normal subjects who related in this way. On the other hand, 80 percent of the normal and only 42 percent of the schizophrenics had close friends.[12] In my study of closest friendships among several samples of college students, I found that from 3 to 6 percent admittedly lacked close friends.[13] Hamilton and Wall, in fact, have pointed out that many schizophrenics never developed the social skills to relate effectively, and hence lacked close friends.[14] Some by their antagonism were ostracized by the group. On a situational level, members of minority ethnic groups in a given neighborhood frequently were excluded from friendships by neighboring peers of the majority ethnic group in the area. This difficulty in forming peer relationships may help explain why members of a minority group in a given local area had higher rates of schizophrenia than those of the majority group.

Estrangement of preschizophrenics from peers was intensified because their internalized parental norms were incompatible with those of their peers.

Many schizophrenics had histories of being "good boys" or "model boys" in the opinion of their parents, especially their demanding mothers. Obedient to their parents, schizophrenics in the lower class came into conflict with their peers. When they refused to fight or engage in body contact sports, they were rejected as "sissies," and began to feel lonely and "different." They either associated with younger boys or retreated to benign and protective relations with adults. Some youths were so viciously taunted and ridiculed that they broke down and had to be hospitalized.

11. L. Wynne, et al., "Pseudo-Mutuality in the Family Relations of Schizophrenia," *Psychiatry* (May, 1958) 21:2:205-220.

12. Melvin Kohn and John Clausen, "Social Isolation and Schizophrenia," *American Sociological Review* (June, 1955), 20:3:266-268.

13. S. Kirson Weinberg, "The Relevance of the Forms of Isolation to Schizophrenia," *International Journal of Social Psychiatry* (Winter, 1966-67) 13:1:33-41.

14. D. W. Hamilton and J. H. Wall, "The Hospital Treatment of Dementia Praecox," *American Journal of Sociology* (September, 1948) 105:3:349-351.

Relations with the Opposite Sex

Since schizophrenics have manifest difficulty with their sexual identity, it is not surprising that their relationships with the opposite sex were observed to be incomplete, transient, frequently filled with conflict, and fragmentary. Many males remained so dependent upon their parents that they did not associate with the opposite sex. This seclusive difficulty accounts for the high rates of male hospitalized schizophrenics (66 percent) who remained single, as reported by Faris and Dunham.[15]

Many adolescent girls during this period of infatuations entered into love liaisons, then, when jilted, could not bear the rejection and broke down.

Marital Relations

Although type of marriage may contribute to the onset of a disorder, the experiences in marital relationships indicate a process of conflict and estrangement between the mates prior to the onset of a breakdown by one of the marital partners. Sampson, Messinger and Towne described this estrangement in analyzing the marital relations of eleven families. They found that marital relationship was characterized by mutual withdrawal and the development of separate worlds of concern. During the early part of the marriage, one of the mates expressed marked discontent with the marriage. This was followed by a period of violent conflict, which resulted in reduced communication and alienation of the mates.[16] As this marital situation continued, each mate encountered the complaints, deviation from routine, worry and irritability of the other mate. A breakout of shouting or aggression then occurred, which the normal mate recognized as a problem beyond control, and realized that the troubled spouse either required psychiatric treatment or had to be sent, forcibly if necessary, to a mental hospital.

SOCIAL FACTORS

Social factors which reflect the social experiences of disordered persons include the place of residence and community, whether urban or rural, as well as the specific local community, the social class and occupation, the age and sex. Generally, information concerning the psychoses is derived from hospital and clinical records and surveys, while information regarding neuroses is derived from surveys and self-reported information.

Urban and Rural Areas

Psychotics, especially schizophrenics, are hospitalized about twice as frequently in urban as in rural areas. Manic-depressive psychoses tend to be hospitalized in approximately identical rates for these two general areas. The discrepancy in ratios may result from differentials in social stress and from variations in social definition of the psychoses. Seemingly, the psychotics can accommodate themselves more easily in rural than in urban areas, are less likely to be pushed into stress situations on a farm than in a crowded tenement or apartment.

Within the urban community, schizophrenics tend to be concentrated in deteriorated and disorganized areas but appear in lesser proportion percentages in the more

15. Robert E. L. Faris and H. Warren Dunham, *Mental Disorders in Urban Areas* (Chicago: University of Chicago Press, 1939), pp. 98-109.

16. Harold Sampson, Sheldon L. Messinger and Robert D. Towne, "Family Processes and Becoming a Mental Patient," *American Journal of Sociology* (July, 1962) 68:88-92.

affluent and organized areas. On the other hand, manic-depressives tend to come from deteriorated as well as organized areas. At one time the residential distribution of the psychoses, in urban communities, fitted a definite pattern: the highest rates of psychoses concentrated near the center of the city with declining rates as one approached the periphery. This pattern was similar to that of the residential pattern for delinquents, for drug addicts, and for suicides.[17]

With references to psychotics, the urban residential distribution of schizophrenics is consistent with the general pattern for psychotics: high rates adjacent to the center of the city and low rates in areas distant from the core of the city. Distribution of manic-depressives has a random residential pattern, with high rates in some areas adjacent to, as well as high rates in areas farther distant from the urban center. The researches of Dunham and Faris, initially conducted in Chicago by sorting 10,575 mental hospital cases, have been corroborated by ecological studies of psychoses generally, and of the different psychoses in Cleveland, Kansas City, Milwaukee, Omaha and St. Louis.[18] These distributions not only indicate the patterned residential distribution of the different psychoses, but also reveal the class position of the psychotics. Schizophrenics tend to concentrate in the lower classes, while the manic-depressives tend to be found in higher as well as lower social classes.

Social Class

In a study of social class determined largely by occupations and education as correlates of mental disorders, Hollingshead and Redlich found that neurotics have the highest rates in the middle and upper classes, and the lowest rates in the lower classes. Psychotics, especially schizophrenics, have the lowest rates in the upper classes, with an increasing rate by declining class position with highest rates in the lowest class. Of psychotics generally, Class IV, the working class, accounted for 38.6 percent, the upper class or Class I, had one percent, while the lowest class V accounted for 36.8 percent. Of schizophrenics, 0.7 of one percent were in the highest class, while 45.2 percent were in the lowest class. Inhibited, intellectually obsessive, and fantasy-ridden neuroses were prevalent among the middle and upper classes. Persons in the lower classes acted out their conflicts, rather than inhibiting them.[19]

Since schizophrenics predominate in the lower classes, the question arises whether they have been reared in this class and have broken down as a result of stresses encountered in poverty, or whether they have drifted downward because they lacked the personal stability and competence to remain in a higher stratum. The results of research are divided, without any necessarily conclusive evidence for either position. Hollingshead and Redlich, Clausen and Kohn, Weinberg, Lepouse and others have found little if any evidence in the course of their research indicating that the schizophrenics are products of downward drift to poverty. On the other hand, Dunham, Goldberg and Morrison, and Gerard, maintain on the basis of their studies, that schizophrenics have drifted downward to the lower classes. Roman and Trice reported that 74 percent of their schizophrenic subjects were native

17. Faris and Dunham, *Mental Disorders*.
18. *Ibid.*
19. August Hollingshead and Frederick C. Redlich, *Social Class and Mental Illness* (New York: John Wiley & Sons, Inc., 1958).

to the poverty segment and 26 percent revealed some degree of downward drift. But this downward mobility was not steep, because most of these subjects descended from Class IV, the working class, to Class V, the lower class.[20] The prevalence of schizophrenia in the lower classes is consistent with the general findings by Srole and his associates concerning clinical well-being and social class. They reported that the highest class has the highest percentage of well or symptom-free persons and the lowest number of impaired persons, while the lowest class has the least number of well persons and the highest percentage of impaired individuals.[21]

The occupational distribution of schizophrenics is consistent with their residential and class pattern. Schizophrenics are concentrated among the unskilled and semi-skilled workers and decline in ratio with ascent on the occupatonal scale. Hence, the fewest schizophrenics were found among the professional and managerial types.[22]

The manic-depressives were distributed more randomly in the occupational structure having a higher proportion than the schizophrenics among the white collar, professional and managerial categories.

Age and Sex

The majority of schizophrenics are admitted into the mental hospital before age 35, while the majority of manic-depressives admitted are older than thirty-five. Thus, since schizophrenia is so prevalent, the majority of patients admitted to mental hospitals are younger than thirty-five. At the other extreme is the large proportion of breakdowns among those who are older than sixty. In fact, an increase of psychoses among the aged remains an increasingly challenging problem, complicated by the

tendency of the children to commit their parents to mental hospitals; recently, however, this has abated somewhat because of sendng the aged to rest homes.[23]

Since 1960, with mounting stress encountered by adolescents, there has been a sharp increase in the incidence of psychoses among this age group, and in their admissions to mental hospitals. In fact this increase has been so marked that many hospitals have had to allocate special wards for youths. Ohio, Illinois, Kansas, California, Pennsylvania, Texas, Virginia and Louisiana have experienced very large increases in the percentages of admissions of patients under age twenty-five.

DIAGNOSIS, DISPOSITION AND TREATMENT

The disposition of the patient assigned to receive treatment or to be committed to a

20. Hollingshead and Redlich, *Ibid*; Kohn and Clausen, "Social Isolation and Schizophrenia"; S. Kirson Weinberg, "Basic Issues in Contemporary Psychiatric Sociology," *Current Trends in Psychiatry*; eds, Paul Roman and Harrison Trice (New York: Science Press, 1974—forthcoming); Rema Lapouse, et al., "The Drift Hypothesis and Socioeconomic Differentials in Schizophrenia," *American Journal of Public Health* (August, 1956), 46:6, pp. 978-986; H. Warren Dunham, et al., "A Research Note on Diagnostic Mental Illness and Social Class," *American Sociological Review* (October, 1966), 31:5, pp. 223-227; Harrison Trice and Paul Roman, *Schizophrenia and Poor* (Ithaca: New York School of Industrial and Labor Relations, 1967); E. M. Goldberg and S. L. Morrison, "Schizophrenia and Social Class" *British Journal of Psychiatry*, (1963) 109:785-802.

21. Leo Srole, et al., *Mental Health in the Metropolis* (New York: McGraw-Hill Book Company, 1962), pp. 159-169, 212-216.

22. Robert Frumkin, "Occupation and the Major Mental Disorders," *Mental Health and Mental Disorders*, ed. Arnold M. Rose (New York: W. W. Norton & Company, Inc., 1955), pp. 136-160.

23. National Institute of Mental Health. *Patients in Mental Institutions, 1962* (Washington D. C.: Government Printing Office, 1963).

mental hospital varies with his or her socio-economic status, as well as with age and family position. A person in the lower class is dealt with in ways different from those used with persons in the middle and upper class. Thus, a person in the lower class eventually will be sent to a state mental hospital, after his agitated condition impels his family to call the police. He may spend a night in the lock-up. He must be given a trial before he can be judged insane or in need of mental treatment; then he may be committed to a mental hospital. The principal reasons for involuntary confinement are the state's right to defend itself from dangerous persons, and to assist those persons who cannot help themselves.[24] An upper middle class person would be sent to a private sanitarium, while the upper class person might receive the special care of a psychiatrst and nurse.

The State Mental Hospital

The state mental hospital is the institution which cares for most of the psychotic patients in the United States. It is called a hospital because the patients are considered mentally ill; but their illness is not equivalent in kind nor parallel to physical illness. Mental hospital patients consist predominantly of people who were initially adjudged by their relatives or other persons in the community as requiring forcible removal from social participation in society.

A mental hospital has several functions. It provides care and custody for its patients. As a treatment center, it serves patients who can respond to therapy. It prevents patients from escaping, and from harming other patients, the staff and themselves. Its ancillary function, which frequently takes top priority, is to provide full and part maintenance for a professional and nonprofessional staff. Many staff persons reside on the hospital grounds so that, together with the patients, the mental hospital comprises a relatively self-contained community.[25]

For many generations, until after World War II, mental hospitals usually were called insane asylums. These institutions were not hospitals at all, but a cross between a prison and a boarding house. Some persons referred to the very large ones as depositories or warehouses where humans were stored for an interim period, or indefinitely. The use of electric shock and drugs enabled patients responsive to such treatment to improve, and these eventually were discharged. Others who were not responsive to treatment were retained indefinitely in the hospital as chronic patients. The longer they remained in the hospital, the less attention they received. Eventually, they were shifted to the back wards, where they were virtually forgotten. Thus the mental hospital was stratified in accordance with the types of patients—hopeful and chronic inmates. In the past the bottom patient category, the agitated patients, comprised a large proportion of the total patients, before the advent of electric-shock and drug-therapy. At present they constitute a small minority of patients, whose agitated condition is usually temporary.

After World War II, the brutal restraints of the inmates such as the strait jacket and ankle chain were discarded as means of controlling agitated patients. Electric-shock

24. Dunham and Weinberg, *Culture of the Mental Hospital.*
25. See S. Kirson Weinberg, *Society and Personality Disorders, op. cit.;* Ivan Belknap, *Human Problems of a State Mental Hospital* (New York: McGraw-Hill Book Company, Inc., 1956).

therapy became an effective therapeutic device for helping agitated patients regain their composure. The use of drugs had an even more positive effect in facilitating the improvement of the patients. The social organization of the mental hospital also changed. It became less rigorous in its restraint of the movements of the patients. Patients were freer to move about. Diminished popular fear and dread of mental hospital patients encouraged the hospital policy of granting to improved patients week-end furloughs prior to their discharge. In brief, the advent of effective physical and drug therapies, the practice of individual psychotherapy and some group therapy, improvement of conditions within the mental hospital, diminution of the dread associated with mental illness, and recognition that patients could be helped by guidance through clinics near or adjacent to their home communities, reversed a trend among resident patients that had been maintained until 1955.[26] Up to that time, the number of resident patients was continually increasing, but after that year their numbers began to decrease annually. This decline in resident patients was not a result of a decline in patient admissions, but was attributable to an increase in patient discharges.

This trend culminated in a movement called "community psychiatry," which was influenced by the sociological approach to prevention, specifically, juvenile delinquency (see Chapter II). This meant that instead of confining the patients within this distant, vast repository called a mental hospital, many patients were sent to half-way houses and nursing homes within the community, where they would be closer and more accessible to their relatives. The acceptance of this attitude/policy of accepting patients in the outside community received an encouraging impetus from the orientation and policies of President Kennedy, who regarded the use of community resources as central to a new approach to the treatment and prevention of mental disorders.[27]

This approach toward rehabilitating mentally disordered persons, as well as preventing mental disorders, has many positive facets but it also claims too much.

Persuant to such a policy, some patients would be placed in half-way houses, in a status between that of being institutionalized and being discharged. Thus the sudden shock of outright release would be eased, with the patients' consequent adjustment facilitated. Within the community the several agencies, social centers, qualified personnel, and programs pertinent to the rehabilitation of the patients, would be used. This policy would also recognize that the reorientation of the family toward the patient would be essential, because the conflict and estrangement very likely have been generated and/or precipitated by family and marital relationships. Many patients who have demonstrated that they are no danger to the community have undoubtedly benefited by this approach.[28] One difficulty, however, has been associated with the private management of the nursing and half-way houses. Although these homes have had to comply with state standards,

26. National Institute of Mental Health. *Patients in Mental Institutions, 1962.*
27. John F. Kennedy, "Mental Illness and Mental Retardation." A message from the President of the United States, February 5, 1963, 1st Session, Document No. 58, p. 1, to the House of Representatives, 88th Congress.
28. Leopold Bellak, ed., *Handbook of Community Psychiatry and Community Mental Health* (New York: Grune and Stratton, 1964).

many operated on the borderline of such standards, with excessive crowding of patients. Perhaps the outside facilities should also be administered by the state.

Resource to the community as a preventive unit implies that the mentally disordered person is recognized as a human being, not a mere organism, and that those persons who show early signs of disorder can be detected and helped by certain measures. We have referred to such symptoms as parent-child conflict as well as estrangement from the peer group as indicators of potential breakdown.

One preventive program, the Woodlawn Mental Health Center in Chicago, strived (1) to relate the social processes in the community to the symptoms of disorder among children, (2) to ascertain the mental health needs of the persons within the community and (3) to determine whether the agencies, personnel and programs are fulfilling these needs.[29]

For Further Reading

Clausen, John A. *Sociology and the Field of Mental Health.* New York: Russel Sage Foundation, 1956.

A review of some relevant aspects and problems of mental disorders from a sociological vantage point.

Dunham, H. Warren and Weinberg, S. Kirson. *Culture of the State Mental Hospital.* Detroit: Wayne State University Press, 1960.

An analysis of the culture and social structure of the state mental hospital. It emphasizes the plight of the patient in the hospital setting.

Hollingshead, August B., and Redlich, Frederick C. *Social Class and Mental Illness.* New York: John Wiley & Sons, Inc., 1958.

A research study of the relationship between social class and types of mental disorder.

Scheff, Thomas J. *Being Mentally Ill: A Sociological Theory.* Chicago: Aldine Publishing Company, 1968.

This book deals with the varied ways in which mental disordered persons are socially defined and the effects of these social definitions.

Weinberg, S. Kirson, ed. *Psychiatric Sociology: The Sociology of Mental Disorders.* Chicago: Aldine Publishing Company, 1967.

A penetrating and complete sociological analysis of the distribution, social processes and factors contributing to disorders and in the definition and efforts in the treatment and prevention of disorders.

29. Sheppard G. Kellam and Sheldon K. Schiff, "An Urban Community Mental Health Center," *Mental Health and Urban Social Policy*, eds. Leonard J. Duhl and Robert J. Leopold (San Francisco: Jossey-Bass, Inc., Publishers, 1968).

6 | Suicide

IN an affluent society, where life is indulgent and comfortable, the act of suicide may evoke surprise and horror. Life seems too pleasant to snuff out by one's own hand, because suicide means the deliberate or even unintentional taking of one's life, or lack of activity necessary to preserve life. Legally defined suicide is regarded as disorderly conduct. From an orthodox religious vantage point suicide is condemned as self-murder. The suicide is a dual actor: the afflicted victim and the homicide. Within the range of acceptable behavior the person, as a member of society, is required to protect his life as well as fulfill his obligations toward those dependent upon him. The overwhelming majority of people prize and defend their lives so intensely that self-preservation is considered a basic motive; it formerly was called an "instinct." In discussing the strange phenomenon of self-murder, this chapter investigates: (1) the extent, (2) types of suicide, (3) the social processes, (4) social factors contributing to suicide, and (5) its control and prevention.

EXTENT OF SUICIDE

Among violent deaths, suicides are second only to automobile accidents, and twice as frequent as rates of homicides: 10.8 to 5.1.[1]

Although official statistics record about 24,000 suicides annually for 1970, the actual count of suicides may be considerably higher. One estimate is as high as 50,000. The official count of suicide would be less than the estimated actual number for several reasons: first, individuals who attempt suicide may not die immediately, but may linger on for days or weeks. When they do succumb, their cause of death may be listed as pneumonia or accident. Second, some suicides, because of family shame or because of insurance requirements, may be listed as a heart attack or an accident, such as a fatal fall. Third, some suicides seem to be consequences of avoidable automobile accidents. Fourth, since suicide is considered a serious sin in some religious groups, death is attributed to another cause. In brief, estimates of suicide vary but are recognized to be higher than the official count.

Types of Suicide

Suicide is classified into two general types: (1) group-coerced, and (2) individually-motivated.

1. United Nations, *Demographic Yearbook*, 1965 (New York: 1966), pp. 762-774.

Group-coerced suicide refers to deaths resulting from voluntary self-sacrifice or death from group pressure and/or group welfare. During World War II, Japanese Kami-Kaze or suicidal pilots dive-bombed American ships and blew themselves up with their planes. A disgraced military officer may prefer the alternative of death by shooting himself, what Durkheim called "obligatory altruistic suicide," rather than endure a stigmatized execution for his offense. In some primitive or nonliterate societies, individuals are selectively designated for sacrifice to appease tribal gods. Generally, in a very cohesive society, collective welfare or survival precedes individual options, because the sanctity of the individual is low in the scale of values. At this level, group-coerced or altruistic suicide, as Durkheim conceived it, results from group pressure demanding a member's direct death or requiring such hazardous activities that his death is very likely.[2]

Individually-motivated suicide which results from personal motives and orientations includes (1) egotistic and (2) anomic types. Egotistic suicide results from isolation and self-hatred. The potential suicide considers his very act of living a long drawn out stretch of boredom, or of recrimination and self-hatred. The strain of enduring intense self-reproach, self-accusation and self-denunciation becomes intolerable.

Anomic suicide results from a loss of social balance, from an abrupt upward or downward shift of status. In this sudden change the individual finds that his social world may become purposeless because he lacks acceptable goals and meaningful social relations. In this social void which he cannot accept, he may develop suicidal tendencies. For example, the individual who

abruptly and unexpectedly loses his wealth rejects his dire, disagreeable, poverty-ridden circumstances and sees death as an outlet. On the other hand, an individual who experiences a relatively sudden socio-economic ascent by inheriting a fortune, or through success as a singer or an author, may find his new position so drastic a change that his former intense strivings and defenses become meaningless aspirations.[3]

THE ESTRANGEMENT PROCESSES IN SUICIDE

What are the processes and motivations which lead persons to suicide? We have indicated some of these motives in characterizing the three types of suicide, but let us elaborate the two types of individual suicide.

Suicidal tendencies develop from early and later social relationships, as well as from an isolated position in the social structure.[4] The conception of isolation as a cause of suicides does not indicate, however, the dynamics of the person's relationships. Thus, the person's inadequate social skills and social relations, combined with critical situations, develop the feelings of loneliness from rejection and the self-hatred from failure, which could precipitate self-destruction.

Suicide thus culminates a social process in which the individual seeks social accep-

2. Emil Durkheim, *Suicide* (New York: The Free Press, 1951).
3. *Ibid.*; Richard H. Serden, *Suicide Among Youth: A Review of the Literature, 1900-1967* (Washington: Joint Commission on Mental Health, Children, 1968).
4. Maurice Farber, *The Theory of Suicide* (New York: Funk and Wagnalls, 1968), pp. 61-65; S. Kirson Weinberg, "The Relevance of the Forms of Isolation to Schizophrenia," *International Journal of Social Psychiatry*, 13:1 (1966-67) pp. 33-41.

tance and affection, yet ultimately has been denied both. He thus feels the futility of life and turns his aggressions against himself. Frequently experiencing isolation with its subjective counterpart of loneliness, he is unable to anchor himself socially because he lacks sustaining social relationships and association with groups among whom he can feel an integral participant. He sees death as an escape if not a "solution" to his conflicts.

His estrangement from other persons or from meaningful activities may be slow or rapid, whether from loss of a job, or decline of his social standing with his family, friends, or colleagues, or because of the death of a loved one. Thus, the individual, unable even in early life to cultivate close social relations, may find himself somewhat removed from others and continually feeling a sense of isolation, from which he may need constant reassurance.

Or he may identify with people who are essentially hostile to him. These people may be his family members who express ambivalent attitudes. On the one hand they claim they want him to succeed but they seem pleased when he fails. Without an explicit understanding of this self-defeating reaction he may seek success too avidly; but he does things to fail. His compensatory reactions may persist in subsequent behavior until he encounters a problem which he cannot solve and cannot endure.

Another type of person who acquires suicidal tendencies develops in an overprotected environment in which he is encouraged to remain immature. He gets his way by immature tantrums, which he continues as a strategy through adolescence and adult life. He resorts to outbursts of anger or to isolated sulking when frustrated in his wishes, and uses these as a means of con-

trolling others. He may resort to attempted suicide when lesser efforts do not elicit the sympathy he seeks. But sometimes his suicidal pretenses do not work out as he anticipates. The other person does not show up on time to rescue him, and death follows.

Suicide also may be the culmination of self-hatred, which results in self-destruction. The dynamics that contribute to depression also, in a more extreme way, impel the suicide. Both the depressive and the suicide are imbued with punitive attitudes toward themselves. Their self-hatred may be mingled with hatred of significant persons who are intimately associated, such as family members, fiancé, friends, employers or teachers, who have been rejective or oppressive. For this reason, homicide may be mingled with suicide. In fact, 4 percent of the suicides precede their self-destructive act by homicide.[5] In this category, suicides are those who strive to kill people at random before commiting suicide. Still others may want to share their death with others and hence destroy persons close to them. On a symbolic level, from a psychoanalytic viewpoint, the suicide's inverted aggression manifests in his own thinking the incorporated hated object or person, such as the parent, mate, or fiancée who has humiliated or insulted him.

Precipitating Situations

People who are about to commit suicide have striven to solve their personal problems, but failed. Desperate and without fur-

5. See Marvin E. Wolfgang, "An Analysis of Homicide-Suicide," *Deviant Behavior and Social Process,* ed. William A. Rushing (Chicago: Rand McNally and Co., 1969), pp. 273-279; D. J. West, *Murder Followed by Suicide* (London: William Heinemann, Ltd., 1965), pp. 17, 28.

ther options, they may begin to feed on thoughts of doing away with themselves. These thoughts are frequently communicated to others. Robins and his associates found that 69 percent of 134 suicides expressed their intentions about death and suicide.[6] Most of their communications denoted anguish, defeat and despair, or the wish to disappear ("You'll never see me again"). Of 26 suicidal ideas indicated, the most frequent were: first, a "statement of intent to commit suicide, second, a reaction of being "better off dead" or "tired of living." Only 5 percent expressed bitterness in their observations.

The initial efforts at suicide may not necessarily be genuine. Schneidman and Farberow reported after an analysis of 221 suicide notes, that the individual who intended to commit suicide wrote a farewell note, or disposed of his property, or did something to indicate the finality of his act. The pretended suicide who does not wish to kill himself but goes through the motions, omits this gesture of impendng fatality. Weiss has reported that the genuine suicide takes measures that cause death rapidly, while the pretended suicide resorts to techniques that proceed slowly, so as to provide time for him to be rescued.

Although a first or second attempt at suicide may not be completed, the prospective suicide may mean it in a subsequent suicidal act.

In general, the use of pills in some form is perhaps the most widespread form of suicide; but men tend to resort to violent means such as firearms more frequently than women. In 1930, Dublin and Bunzel reported that of about 57,000 white male suicides, 60.5 percent shot or hanged themselves, while of about 17,000 white females, 53 percent used poison or gas. At present,

females predominantly resort to pills as do men, but the general tendency among male suicides is to resort to violent means of death more frequently than women.[7] Women have higher rates of attempted suicide than men, but men have higher rates of completed suicide. Some attribute this discrepancy to the fact that women more frequently desire attention and sympathy; but another view is that women simply have less knowledge of how to commit suicide than men do.[8]

SOCIAL ORGANIZATION AND SUICIDE

Loosely organized societies which lack social cohesion have higher rates of individualized suicide than cohesive societies. In fact, indicators of types of groups or social categories of degrees of social cohesion reveal higher rates of suicide among the less cohesive units. Thus urban communities have higher suicide rates than rural communities, Protestant denominations than Catholics, residents of hotel or rooming houses than those in single-home family residential areas, divorced more than married or widowed and persons older than age 65 than married men younger than age 65.[9] Durkheim emphasized that when

6. Eli Robins, Seymour Gassner, Jack Kayes, Robert Wilkinson and George Murphy, "The Communication of Suicidal Interest: 134 Consecutive Cases of Successful (Completed) Suicide," *American Journal of Psychiatry*, 115 (1959), pp. 724-733.

7. Louis Dublin and Bessie Bunzel, *To Be or Not To Be* (New York: Smith and Haas, 1933).

8. See James Wilkins, "Suicidal Behavior," *American Sociological Review*, 32:2 (April, 1967), pp. 286-298.

9. Andrew F. Henry and James F. Short, Jr., *Suicide and Homicide* (New York: The Free Press, 1954).

society is strongly organized it holds its members under its controls, considers them of service, and forbids them to deviate by disposing of themselves. Thus social control gives the individual a life of meaning through conformity. In loosely cohesive societies the members can deviate and become estranged from the control of societal norms, and one way they do so is by disposing of themselves through suicide.[10] Thus the disorganized society which involves the declining control over its members may have higher suicide rates than the organized society. On this level, Gibbs and Martin have attempted to relate the degree of social organization of a group, community or society with suicide. They maintain that the suicide rates vary inversely with the stable and durable social relations in a society. These stable social relations vary with the degree to which the members conform to its cultural imperatives. But their degree of conformity to these imperatives varies inversely with the extent to which they confront role-conflict by reason of incompatible statuses.[11]

SOCIAL FACTORS INFLUENCING SUICIDE

What social factors contribute to high rates of suicide?

Urban-Rural

Rates of suicide tend to be one-third higher in urban than rural areas. Furthermore, although suicide rates tend to increase with size of city, the largest metropolitan centers, except for Los Angeles, do not have the highest suicide rates. New York, Chicago or Boston are not ranked among the top ten cities with the highest suicide rates. Suicide rates are undoubtedly influenced by the age composition of the population. Los Angeles, St. Petersburg and Miami have high suicide rates because of the high proportions of aged people, who are prone to suicide.

Porterfield and Talbert compared the suicides and homicides in 43 southern and 43 nonsouthern cities. They found that nonsouthern cities had 3.6 times as many suicides as homicides while southern cities had 1.7 times as many homicides as suicides.[12]

Race

Blacks in the south during the time of caste repression had very low rates of suicide, but very high rates of homicide. As blacks migrated to northern cities and were incorporated into the competitive working class and middle class structure, they began to experience new kinds of stress and to incorporate the dynamics of self-blame that can motivate suicide. Thus their suicide rates increased. In 1929, the blacks had the lowest suicide rate of all races, 4.1 per 100,000 of the general black population as compared with the white rate of 15 per 100,000 among the general white population.[13]

In comparing the changing suicide rates from 1952-53 to 1962-63, it is evident that

10. Emil Durkheim, *Suicide*.

11. Jack P. Gibbs and Walter T. Martin, "A Theory of Status Integration and Its Relationship to Suicide," *American Sociological Review*, 23.2 (April, 1958), pp. 142-144.

12. Austin L. Porterfield and Robert H. Talbert, *Crime, Suicide and Social Well-Being in Your State and City* (Forth Worth: Leo Potishman Foundation, 1968), pp. 98-101; see also Ronald W. Maris, *Social Forces in Urban Suicide* (Homewood, Illinois: Dorsey Press, 1969).

13. Dublin and Bunzel, *To Be or Not To Be*; Louis Dublin, *Suicide: A Sociological and Statistical Study* (New York: Ronald Press, 1963).

while the blacks have a lower suicide rate per 100,000 of the same general population than the whites, their percentage for increase of suicides is higher than whites for each age category.[14]

Urban Areas

Mobile, transient and nonfamily urban areas have the highest suicide rates in the metropolitan community. The distribution of suicides in Chicago, Minneapolis, and Seattle shows the highest rates in nonfamily areas such as the central business district of hotels and skid-row slum areas, and the lowest rates in family residential areas.[15] Sainsbury, who has studied the ecological distribution of suicides in London, emphasized that the most influential factors in suicide were social isolation, social mobility, and social disorganization. In the rooming and boarding house boroughs of London he found considerable isolation, loneliness, and mobility. He inferred that the large turnover of residents not only revealed a situational influence in which residents could not cultivate sustained social relations, but that a selective process also operated in which the mobile and dissatisfied persons gravitated to these areas.[16]

Sex and Age

Men commit suicide more frequently than women. The rates for men increase with age, while the suicide rates for women increase until they reach age 45, after which their rates of suicide decline. In Seattle, for example, the suicide rates for males was 37.8 per 100,000, while for women it was 12.4 per 100,000. On the other hand, women have higher rates of attempted suicide than men. One hypothesis is that men commit suicide more frequently than women be-

cause of increased stress they encounter, particularly between the ages of 40 to 55.[17] Although women encounter less direct stress than men, they are, according to Wilkins, more ignorant than men about the ways of commiting suicide and hence have higher rates of attempted suicide.[18]

Age

Children under 9 rarely commit suicide, while persons age 65 and older have very high rates of suicide. Adolescents, who in the past have had relatively low rates of suicide, recently have increased markedly in the percentage of suicides, as have their rates of mental disorder. The patterns of suicide for the sexes vary by age. Men tend to have an increasingly higher rate of suicide as they grow older, while women have increasing rates of suicide only until age 45 when their rates begin to decline. But for the general population suicides increase with age. The higher number of suicides for a given age period is between 45 to 54 for males, a situation which may be a reaction of failure and self-reproach characteristic of egotistic suicide. But males age 65 and older have the highest rates of suicide.

14. Herbert Hendin, *Black Suicide* (New York: Basic Books, Inc., Publishers, 1969).

15. Calvin F. Schmid and Maurice F. Van Arsdol, Jr., "Completed and Attempted Suicides: A Comparative Analysis," *American Sociological Review*, 20:3 (June, 1955), pp. 273-283.

16. Peter Sainsbury, *Suicide in London* (New York: Basic Books Inc., Publishers, 1955), pp. 72-80.

17. Calvin F. Schmid, *Suicide in Seattle, 1914-1925: An Ecological and Behavioristic Study* (Seattle: University of Washington Publications in the Social Sciences, 1928); see also Federal Security Agency, *Deaths and Death Rates for Selected Causes by Age, Race and Sex* (Washington, D. C.: U.S. Government Printing Office, 1948).

18. James F. Wilkins, "Suicidal Behavior."

They have been forced to retire, are in effect removed from their former positions of importance, and reluctantly enter a way of life that is essentially purposeless to them. In this predicament they may resort to suicide as a way out of an oppressive anomic condition. At the other end of the age spectrum, the increase of suicides among adolescents indicates the mounting stresses which they are compelled to encounter. From 1952-53 to 1962-63, youths aged 15 to 24 showed a percentage increase of 35 percent among whites and 80 percent among blacks. In roughly that same span, the percentage of suicide deaths for persons under age 20 rose from 2.02 to 3.24. Among youths, age 15 to 24, suicide ranks as the fifth of the causes of death, behind accidents, malignancies, cardiovascular-renal diseases, and homicides.[19]

Occupation and Social Class

The relevance of occupation and social class to suicide remains inconclusive as, reflected in diverse findings of the several studies. First Powell in a study of suicide in Tulsa, Oklahoma found that the occupational distribution of suicides formed a U-shaped curve. The suicide rates were highest at both ends of the occupational spectrum, at the top, among the professional and managerial and at the bottom, among the unskilled workers, while the clerical-sales, semi-skilled and skilled workers had the lowest suicide rates. Persons at these diverse extremes committed suicide for different reasons and in different ways. The upper middle and upper class persons resorted to suicide in desperation and after deliberation, when they could no longer sustain their appearance of success. The lower class persons, in moods of random and irrational aggression, lashed out at others and at themselves, with fatal results.[20]

A study in England reported that professionals had the highest rates of suicide, while the unskilled workers had the lowest rates of suicide. On the other hand, a study of suicides in Cook County (which is composed largely of Chicago) reported that the unskilled workers had the highest suicide rates, which declined inversely with one's rise in the occupational scale, so that the professionals in the upper class had the lowest suicide rates.[21] Apart from national differences of occupational adjustment between England and the United States it appears that these discrepancies are real and remain to be resolved.

Marital Status

Divorce as indicative of marital estrangement and strain tends to involve the highest rates of suicide among those in this marital status, rather than among the widowed, the single, and the married persons. This last category tends to have the lowest rates of suicide. Schmid and Van Arsdol reported that in Seattle divorced males and females had the highest standardized rates of suicide, which were respectively 102 and 30 per 100,000 of the general population of the same sex. Also, divorced persons tend to have higher rates of suicide as they advance in age.[22]

19. Richard H. Seiden, *Suicide Among Youth,* pp. 24-39.

20. Elwin Powell, "Occupation, Status and Suicide," *American Sociological Review,* 23:2 (April, 1958), pp. 136-139.

21. See Sainsbury, "Suicide in London."

22. Schmid and Van Arsdol, "Completed and Attempted Suicides"; *New York Times* (October 8, 1967), Section E, p. 6.

Trends of Suicide

Suicide rates have increased as a long-term trend from 1910 to 1964, with upward fluctuations during economic depressions, especially that of 1930-32 and downward fluctuations during periods of prosperity and of war. Although suicide rates should rise with the spread of urbanization, which has been consistent during this broad interval, the suicide rates actually declined from 1910 to 1920, then rose until 1930, but declined steadily to 1950, with a slight upward shift to 1964, as can be seen in Figure 6.1.[23]

CONTROL AND PREVENTION

The irony of suicide or even of the attempted suicide is that he strives to punish himself. Consequently, any societal effort to add to the punishment should he fail to die would obviously be a contradiction. The contemporary emphasis is to strive to identify the potential suicide and somehow to reach him before he carries out the fatal act. Thus the effort at prevention means to reach out to the one who is ambivalent about self-destruction and who seeks help. To speak of the prevention of suicide in terms of minimizing its incidence involves a change in child-rearing practices. It would assume a world which developed mature persons who would be able to confront and to live with their failures. To speak of reducing suicide rates in contemporary, success-oriented society would necessarily involve revising the credo and ethos of the society. For by its distinctions and emphases, success implies many failures. The reward system for achievement and upward mobility would have to be revised, with failures tolerated and accepted. Since aggression is so wide spread and so frequently visible, the upsurge of inhibition and the

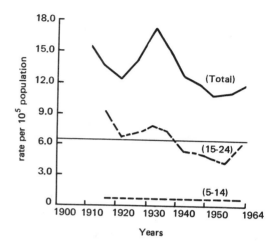

Death Rates for Suicide, White, Both Sexes, United States, 1910-1964 Years

Rate Per 10⁵ Population

Figure 6.1

Source: *Suicide Among Youth: A Review of the Literature: 1900-1967.* Richard H. Seiden. Prepared for the Joint Commission on Mental Health of Children. Task Force III. Figure 6.

absence of aggression would have to be more frequently sought. Even though aggression is outward in contrast to the inverted aggression of the suicide, inward aggression and suicide are consistent when the person encounters failure, rejection and social estrangement.[24]

Prevention Agencies

Institutionalized Agencies to prevent suicide have been very few, and these are lo-

23. Richard H. Seiden, *Suicide Among Youth,* p. 13.
24. Seidin, *"Suicide Among Youth"* pp. 41-46; Karl Menninger, *Man Against Himself* (Harcourt, Brace and Jovanovich, 1938).

73

cated in a few large cities. Such agencies were voluntary associations usually sponsored by religious groups. For example, *Rescue, Incorporated,* sponsored by the Catholic Church, was founded in Boston in 1959; it operated an emergency rescue telephone service which was open 24 hours daily. In addition, the agency enlisted the cooperation of the police and fire department. It afforded counselling and practiced a kind of group therapy in a unit called "Suicides Anonymous." The agency claimed to have helped about 800 persons during 1959. This and other agencies, however humanitarian, lacked the professional skills of the Suicide Prevention Centers (SPC).[25]

The Suicide Prevention Centers were the outcome of concerted research, mainly by Farberow and Schneidman, who applied the results of their research to preventive action. These SPC's used several approaches in dealing with potential and or attempted suicides. They surveyed the files of physicians, general hospitals, and mental hospitals in the area for potential suicides. They used this information as a cumulative fund which they combined with information from the relatives and close friends of suicides. These Suicide Prevention Centers which have spread throughout the United States, are located mainly in large cities and provide mainly a 24 hour a day, 365 day a year emergency telephone service. The agencies also consult professionals such as

physicians, nurses, social workers, and are assisted by trained volunteers.[26]

For Further Reading

Durkheim, Emile. *Suicide.* New York: The Free Press, 1951. Trans. by John A. Spaulding and George Simpson.
    This enduring study of suicide has been the basis for the sociological orientations in the analysis of the types of suicide and the social factors contributing to suicide.
Farberow, Norman L. and Schneidman, Edwin S., eds. *The Cry for Help.* New York: McGraw-Hill Book Company, 1961.
    This action-oriented selection of articles deals with the modes of detecting suicides as well as understanding the symptoms that may be indicative of the conflicts of suicide.
Haughton, Anson. "Suicide Prevention Programs in the United States—An Overview," *Bulletin of Suicidology,* (July, 1968), pp. 25-29.
    A survey of the developing suicide centers for the prevention of suicides by providing help to attempted suicides.
Henry, Andrew F., and Short, James F., Jr. *Suicide and Homicide.* New York: The Free Press, 1954.
    This elaborate statistical study indicates the varying factors which contribute to suicide. One central hypothesis of suicide is that frustration-aggression may help explain certain types of suicide.

25. Anson Haughton, "Suicide Prevention Programs in the United States—an Overview." *Bulletin of Suicidology* (July, 1968), pp. 25-29.
26. Farberow and Schneidman, *The Cry for Help* (New York: McGraw-Hill Book Co., 1961).

Glossary

Alienation—A process of detachment and estrangement from others and from the established institutions and values. It refers to an individual's being outside the main social groups and institutions and to being powerless to change them.

Anomie—Literally, it means social void. Sociologically it refers to social purposelessness or normlessness in a society. As a result, the individual member lacks standards to organize his behavior toward goals as ends of actions. It refers also to a normlessness of means to attain certain goals, such as success, within American society, and to the recourses to any means, legitimate or illegitimate, to attain one's aspired goals.

Anxiety—A panic reaction to one or a series of threatening stimuli and situations to which the individual is helplessly unable to respond effectively. This helplessness is the basis for a neurotic condition. The psychological efforts at avoiding the threatening situation constitute the neuroses. (See also Mental Disorders.)

Contraculture—Values, orientations, and techniques of a specialized group in conflict with and/or whose members may prey upon the larger society. A particular type of subculture. (See also subculture.)

Corrections—The orientations and techniques involved in striving to change an offender in the prison or on probation, to a law-abiding participant in society. This effort represents an ideal because many prisons have minimal facilities for rehabilitation and emphasize the security of the prison. (See also rehabilitation.)

Deviant Behavior—Refers to a category of actions which are defined by the members of society as being beyond the limits of tolerance and as having violated societal norms.

Drug (opiate) Addiction—The process of uncontrollably craving opiates, especially heroin. This is a binding craving which the afflicted person cannot moderate. Because of his cravings he organizes his routine and changes his life-style to obtain money for the drug. Frequently he deviates from the law by stealing, while the female addict may resort to prostitution as well as thievery.

Half-Way House—An intermediate institution to which an inmate of a mental hospital or of a prison is discharged in order to accustom him, and to facilitate his adjustment, to the outside community.

Homosexuality—The sexual preference of a person for one of the same gender coupled with sexual indifference or aversion to the opposite sex. This departure from heterosexual norms may lead to the organization of one's social routine and association with those of similar sexual preferences.

Identity—Pertains to a self definition from one's social role and from the social definitions he internalizes. A person who is downgraded because of deviant behavior such as by mental illness or criminality acquires a stigmatized identity. But members of deviant groups also acquire an identity which they may rationalize and defend, and within the scheme of their inverse values regard with pride rather than shame.

Juvenile Delinquency—The violation of a law by one under a given age as specified by the particular state. It differs from anti-social behavior which may not necessarily violate the law.

Mental Disorder—A psychological impairment of personality and social behavior, resulting in extreme disorganization which may be caused by organic pathology or by personality conflicts. The broad categories of mental disorders are neuroses, psychoses and psychopathies or acting-out disorders.

Norms—Standards of behavior which are shared by the members of a group as the guidelines of their expected activity.

Rehabilitation—A process by which a law-violating person reorients himself to law-abiding views and can check his impulses to deviant behavior. On a positive level, his attitudes are disposed toward constructive activities within the community, and toward a mode of life which operates within the orbit of societal rules and laws. (See also corrections.)

Role—The part and function one has in the group. Thus, the group deviant has a specific role in the group to which he is compelled to abide. (See also identity.)

Social Control—The processes by which persons conform to the norms and values of a group, community, or society. Informal control refers to the processes of conformity resulting from the presence of known members of the family, peer group and neighbors. Formal control refers to indirect enforcement of conformity through formal agencies such as the police.

Social Disorganization—A disruption of the group or community organization, resulting in the declining control of its members. The declining control, as a consequence of inter-group conflict means that the deviant group members disregard the norms of the larger community and abide by the norms of the deviant group. It also means that solitary individuals deviate as a consequence of their social influences.

Social Problem—A condition or mode of behavior socially defined as objectionable or threatening by the members of a group, community, or society who strive to cope with or to solve the problem by policies, programs and experiments, but are not completely effective. The problem lingers until effective social action can control it. In contemporary society, social problems are usually not eliminated. But when the rates indicating the prevalence of social problems decline, it means effective action programs are applied.

Social Process—The reciprocal influences emerging from social interaction whether between groups or persons. When social relations are positive, social agreement and social acceptance accrue. When special relations are negative, social conflict and social disapproval arise. Generally the social process denotes the dynamics of social interaction.

Stereotype—An overlay of traits upon an individual as a hostile group member. It results from inter-group conflict in which members of an opposing group are considered an out-group and depreciated to justify their being placed in an inferior role and in being exploited, abused, or discriminated. It obscures individual difference, and is an expression of social estrangement.

Stigma—A derogatory social label which refers to the person's negative traits or experiences, and which results in his undesirable self-conception by the group. The deviant who is stigmatized may be ostracised from a job as well as rejected by social participation.

Subculture—Distinct sets of values and norms of a specialized group within the larger society, which are transmitted to new members who abide by and sustain its norms and values. (See also contraculture.)

Suicide—The deliberate and voluntary taking of one's life, which in its passive aspects result in not taking measures to protect one's life.

Index

anomie:
  dynamics of, 5
  drug addiction and, 21, 35, 36
  juvenile delinquency and, 19, 25
  suicide and, 66, 67
Ausubel, David P., 2, 31, 33, 37, 42

Becker, Howard S., 1, 10, 15
broken home:
  defined, 25
  juvenile delinquency and, 25, 26
Belknap, Ivan, 62
Bellak, Leopold, 63
Bell, Robert R., 44
Bene, Eva, 46
Bronner, Augusta, 23
Brown, Edward M., 33
Bunzel, Bessie, 68, 69

Cavan, Ruth S., 4, 16, 25
Chein, Isidor, 33, 35, 36
Clausen, John, 58, 64
Clinard, Marshall B., 15, 36
Cloward, Richard, 19, 21, 25, 29, 36
Cohen, Albert K., 3, 5, 20
Coles, Robert, 30, 42
contra-culture. *See also* subculture.
  defined, 4, 5
  deviance and, 4, 5
  drug usage and, 35
  homosexuality and, 50-52
  juvenile delinquency, 19-21
Cressey, Donald, 5, 41

Dal, Bingham, 36
Dank, Harry M., 44, 47, 48, 50, 51, 52
Despert, Louise, 57
deviance. *See also* deviants.
  approaches to, 2, 3
  defined, 1, 2
  labeling theory of, 12

neo-symbolic interaction theory of, 12
rehabilitation of social factors in, 5, 6
social processes in, 1-5
symbolic interaction theory of, 12
types of, 1, 3, 8, 9, 10
deviants. *See also* deviance
  drug addicts as, 37, 38
  group, 2
  homosexuals as, 44, 45
  juvenile delinquents as, 19-21
  mentally disordered as, 53, 54
  primary, 10
  secondary, 10, 11
  solitary, 2, 3, 7
disorganization:
  personal, 2, 3, 23, 24, 46, 47, 67, 68
  social, 5, 6, 24
Douglas, Jack, 3
drugs:
  addiction to, 33, 34
  estrangement and, 35, 36
  extent of usage of, 31, 32
  marihuana as, 42
  personality traits of users of, 37, 38
  prevention of usage of, 41
  social problem of, 38
  subculture of, 34, 35
  suppression of traffic in, 41
  synanon as therapy of, 40, 41
  therapy at, 32, 38, 41
Dublin, Louis, 68, 69
Dunham, H. Warren, 6, 55, 59, 60, 62, 64, 68
Durkheim, Emile, 6, 66, 69, 73

Erickson, Kai T., 1, 10
estrangement:
  defined, 2
  drug, addiction and, 36, 37
  homosexuality and, 46, 47
  juvenile delinquency and, 22
  mental disorders and, 58, 59